MW00716831

TABLE OF CONTENTS

In loving memory of our beloved son, Peter (Perica).
Vecnaja pamjat!

INTRODUCTION

> *Dobar pastir sto kazuje drugom;*
> *on to potvrdjuje svojim djelom!*
>
> *"What a good shepherd advises*
> *others, he confirms with his life."*

The following pages make available to the general reader a number of edifying writings carefully selected from the vast collection of spiritual reflections faithfully produced and submitted by the Very Reverend Protostavrophor Fr. Vojislav Dosenovich for the readers of *Omaha Serbian News*. This collection begins with the June 1955 issue and thus represents half a century of Fr. Dosenovich's pastoral wisdom and guidance.

Obviously not every issue can be represented here, for the number of pages that Father Dosenovich has penned over the decades would indeed make this volume impractical and cumbersome. The following excerpts have been carefully selected and edited into what the editor deems to be the essential best of Father Dosenovich's intellectual and spiritual productivity. Admittedly, some minor editing of these selected writings has taken place; but the reader may be assured that every effort has been made to preserve the integrity and spirit of Father Dosenovich's original thought and writing.

One is invited in the pages that follow to move forward through the Church's yearly cyclical calendar, experiencing renewal through her fasts, savoring her feasts, and accumulating along the way fascinating knowledge and insight about the Orthodox tradition in light of the profound richness of Serbian faith and culture. The process of working through these writings has been personally rewarding and spiritually enriching for me. I trust that the reader will experience the same.

Nicolae Roddy, PhD
January 1, 2004

ABOUT THE AUTHOR

Reverend Father Vojislav Dosenovich grew up in the picturesque but fated region of Bosnia where he witnessed firsthand the atrocities and terrors that ravaged the former Yugoslavia during the Second World War. A graduate of the Orthodox Theological Seminary in Sarajevo, young Vojin, as he was then known, began teaching religion in the public school system just before the war began. Within months following the outbreak of hostilities, the young teacher endured numerous untold sufferings, including the murder of his father, the internment and subsequent death of his only sister, Radojka, and the brutal murders of several brothers, the last of which occurring only recently, in the mid-1990s, during the bloody ethnic wars of Yugoslavia's dissolution.

A young theologian and man of peace, young Vojin was caught in the vise between the powerfully demonic but ultimately doomed ideologies of fascism and communism, from which he barely managed to escape with his life. In 1948, by the will of God, he made his way to the United States where he began working at once in assisting the Serbian Orthodox Church with the task of fulfilling the needs of fellow refugees. It was during that time that he met and soon married the former Nadine Zarajic, received ordination to the Holy Priesthood, and accepted the challenge of a small parish in Omaha, Nebraska. St. Nicholas Serbian Orthodox Church is a modest but faithful congregation that Father Dosenovich has devotedly served for well into a sixth decade now. Throughout this time he has baptized, married, touched the lives, and buried so many members of his flock. A living example of faithfulness and patience, Fr. Dosenovich embodies the essence of that old Serbian proverb, *On obicno daje dobru propovjed, ali njegov zivot je njegova najblja propovjed!* "He usually delivers a good sermon, but his life is his best sermon!"

During his many years in Omaha, Fr. Dosenovich continued building upon the fine education he had received in the former Yugoslavia, earning M.A. degrees in both sociology and psychology from the University of Omaha (now the University of Nebraska at Omaha), followed by Ph.D. studies at the University of Kansas. He has since authored numerous books and articles, including an insightful but unfortunately yet unpublished treatise on the thought of Nikolai Berdyaev, a monograph collection of 62 homilies gathered under the title *Spiritual Reminder*, the informative *On Our Faith,* and the devotional *Feed My Sheep* and *Lord, Teach Us How to Pray.* Last, but certainly far from least, Fr. Dosenovich is also the author of *So Help Me God*, a largely autobiographical work set against the backdrop of war-torn Yugoslavia (1992), an excerpt of which has been reprinted in Chapter Five of this volume.

ABOUT THE EDITOR

Nicolae Roddy is a professor of Old Testament at Creighton University in Omaha, Nebraska, and serves as a co-director for the Bethsaida Excavations Project in Israel. He holds the M.A. in Orthodox Theology from St. Vladimir's Orthodox Theological Seminary in Crestwood, NY, where he studied under the academic and spiritual guidance of Fr. John Meyendorff, of blessed memory, and completed his doctoral studies in 1999, at the University of Iowa. Roddy is the author of *The Romanian Version of the Testament of Abraham: Text, Translation, and Cultural Context* (Atlanta, GA: Society of Biblical Literature, 2001), as well as numerous scholarly and popular articles. Roddy regularly delivers scholarly presentations throughout the country and has also lectured in Romania, Israel, Berlin, and Rome. Of Romanian heritage, Roddy is a member of St. Nicholas Serbian Orthodox Church in Omaha, Nebraska. He and his wife Michelle are raising three children: Aurelia, Eli, and Alexandru.

CHAPTER ONE

EVERYDAY LIVING

ON WORSHIP

Worship is one of the highest and most authentically holy acts one can perform. The impulse to worship God is natural, even universal, but the method for worship must be acquired. The correct method is that which allows the fullest expression of the natural impulse. If the natural impulse is not encouraged in childhood, it tends to decline over time; however it can reawaken even after long neglect. The natural inclination is fostered by training very young children to acquire an experience of God suited to their years, using methods and materials appropriate to their level and patterns of thinking. Whatever the level, through it all there should be simplicity, sincerity, and reverence in harmony with the elemental truth that worship is an act of the soul in its relationship with God.

As we know, gathering together on Sunday morning is the most important time of the week for the community, because it is the public acknowledgment of the primacy of God and an open witness of the community of faith. It is the obligation of every Orthodox Christian to participate in the worship service. Church members should realize that such participation is not an elective duty. Neglecting this obligation weakens God's Church and undermines right living.

Some people claim that it is possible to grow in Christian understanding apart from the Church, but this is a hazardous undertaking and is rarely, if ever, successful. It is our duty to worship God in truth, witnessing our faith in Him through regular participation in our worship services.

June, 1955

THE POWER OF FAITH

"Whosoever shall say unto this mountain, 'Be thou removed and be thou cast into the sea," and shall not doubt in his heart, but shall believe in his heart that those things which he saith shall come to pass; he shall have whatsoever he saith" (Mark 11:23).

Almost by itself can this passage revolutionize one's life by changing defeat into victory. Whatever the "mountain," or tremendous barrier, that stands in the way, it can be broken down and removed from your life. Pray that your mountainous difficulties be removed; as you pray, believe that what you pray is being done, allowing not a doubt nor any negative thought to exist in your mind. Do not have the vague idea that the "mountain" might be removed at some future time, but believe that God is removing it for you then and there.

October, 1958

VICTORY IN THE LORD

"Trust in the Lord with all thine heart and lean not unto thine own understanding."

This text will help anyone avoid any sort of nervous breakdown, or stimulate recovery for one who has experienced one. A famous neurologist often prescribes this text for his patients, writing these words on a card and instructing his patients to say them and commit them to memory so that they become indelibly imprinted on the subconscious mind.

The cause of much nervous trouble is frustration. The antidote for frustration is a calm faith, not in one's own cleverness or hard toil, but in God's guidance. The cure for frustration is belief that God will grant you what you need. Trust in God with all your heart and you will be able to keep working in health and happiness for many years to come. "If God be for us, who can be against us?"

November, 1958

STRESS

Stress can be one of the most oppressive depressants of the spirit. A prolonged, fast-paced pattern of living rapidly drains our energy, leaving our spirits sluggish and dull. Our stress can often be self-imposed, or it can be caused by others. Either way, we suffer the loss of our inner peace.

In order to overcome stress, the mind needs to experience the depth of quietude. One of the most effective passages for producing such a state of mind is this: "Be still and know that I am God" (Psalm 46:10). What an effective relaxation technique, to "be still," that is, reducing our headlong rush into often needless sorts of activities and handing over all our worries to God. Imagine not only slowing down our walking and talking, but coming to a stop altogether! It is necessary that we do this from time to time, for when we are nervous and agitated we are momentarily incapable of those basic creative thoughts that reorganize and refresh our purposeful activity.

So sit still, be silent, and let composure creep over you. Having attained an attitude of stillness, the greatest of all thoughts will be able to occupy your mind, namely to "know that I am God." Realize that you cannot do everything and that the world does not need to rest upon your shoulders. The simple truth that we are only to do our best and leave the rest to God comes back into our consciousness, restoring our soul and lifting our spirits.

November, 1959

WITH WINGS LIKE EAGLES

"But those who wait for the Lord shall renew their strength, they shall mount up with wings like eagles, and they shall run and not be weary, they shall walk and not faint" (Isaiah 40:31). This beautiful passage describes the greatest experience a human being could ever have, a truly spiritual state that one may experience only by surrendering completely to God and entering into his presence. Suddenly the heavy burdens of life fall away as you are lifted up to the highest levels of inner freedom and power.

We realize that no one can permanently sustain such a life, but the experience demonstrates that it can be repeated throughout life, so that we may "run and not be weary." Even when confronted by day-to-day situations that appear to us to be monotonous and difficult, we may acquire power that prevents us from depleting our strength, lifting us to new levels and fueling us with an endless supply of ability. "In Him we live and move and have our being" (Acts 17:28).

We owe our existence to God for we and our lives belong to God. What do we have that does not belong to Him? What has any nation that does not belong to Him, the Creator of All? Knowledge and remembrance of this helps us to maintain our physical, mental, and spiritual energies. The tensions and pressures of modern living weigh heavily upon us, depleting our energy, but we have a means for renewing it. This biblical passage reminds us that God created us and that He can continually recreate us.

The secret is to maintain contact with God, Who channels vitality into our being and constantly replenishes our physical, mental, and spiritual energies. Being in God also ensures that we will be healthy and strong morally as well, which leads to a life of inner peace and love. It would be of benefit if we memorized this verse and repeated it every day.

July, 1960

DEPENDENCE UPON CHRIST

You may ask, how can one face the many personal problems and difficulties of today, whether in the family, on the job, or in society in general? Perhaps your burdens have become greater than your ability to cope with them, an experience faced by many people today. Facing all of these burdens alone would certainly be overwhelming, but bringing our problems to Christ enables us to overcome them.

We read in the Bible of the marvelous things Jesus did for the people, wishing that the same experiences of comfort and healing could be ours. Those who encountered Christ were able to realize astonishing things, to be rescued from plights and gain tremendous advantage over all their difficulties. "Why can't that happen to me?" we sadly ask. But it can!

St. Paul urges us to meditate upon this important saying, "Jesus Christ is the same yesterday and today and forever" (Hebrews 13:8). The Apostle reminds us that Jesus Christ never changes, an unchanging constant in an ever-changing world. God is not a prisoner of time and space, but remains the same now as He was when He walked the shores of the Sea of Galilee. He shows the same loving kindness and the same power to change and heal people's lives. He is the same restorer of courage and transformer of souls. He is as alive today as He was on the way to Golgotha, betrayed by us, and suffering all our doubt and disbelief.

Whatever Christ did for anyone in history He can do for you now. It depends only upon how completely you surrender yourself to Him and how sincerely you believe. Let us pray that God helps us to overcome doubt and unbelief, and that sincere belief takes command of our being in order that we may be in the presence of the ever-living God, the Source of our happiness and peace, our strength and courage, our success and eternal life. Amen.

August, 1960

SEEKING THE KINGDOM OF GOD

Much of our effort these days is directed toward the goal of obtaining security. Indeed, there are many things we want to be secure from. Many of us use every means possible to obtain a certain goal, often missing the goal and hurting ourselves or others, thereby losing our most important security: inner peace.

We want the best things for ourselves, which is the right thing to work for, but often along the way we become misguided, settling for things that are far inferior to that which God would have us enjoy. We must strive for things of real value, which will make our lives rich indeed, including a right attitude that brings peace and good relations with others, and so many other benefits besides. As the Gospel says, "But strive first for the Kingdom of God and his righteousness, and all these things will be given to you as well" (Matt. 6:33).

Each Sunday the priest begins the Divine Liturgy with these words: "Blessed is the Kingdom of the Father and the Son and the Holy Spirit," words that invoke all the blessings of God's Kingdom, which we enjoy already in part. Just what is the Kingdom of God? It is the dominion to which belongs our very existence, whatever the human mind can comprehend, all the nations of the earth, indeed all the world and the farthest reaches of the universe. All strength and power that sustains our lives in integrity, security, goodness, faith, and love emanates from the Kingdom of God. We are invited simply to ask for it, that all of these things may come our way.

Notice that we are also urged to seek God's righteousness. If God has asked us through the Scriptures to do this, then it is something that can be done. In developing our own right-mindedness, by practicing right thinking, we increase things that are good and right for ourselves and for others as well, producing such things as kindness, generosity, gratitude, and understanding.

Let us agree to do the things suggested in this Gospel verse and test the promise that "these things," that is, everything required for a good and happy life, will be added to us. God, who is Life and Love, gave us this instruction out of His boundless love and concern for us, but it depends upon our willingness to receive it and apply it to our lives.

September, 1960

ACQUIRING NEW STRENGTH

Many people often feel that their strength is about to fail and that perhaps even life itself is drawing to an end, as the problems and complexities of life press heavy upon them. Indeed, there are many real challenges to be faced, but it has often been observed that God does not give us burdens too great for us to bear. In times when our strength has been depleted and the vitality is gone from our lives, we should remember that our energy may be renewed and our power to live restored, as the Bible says: "He gives power to the faint, and strengthens the powerless" (Isaiah 40:29).

Whenever we feel that we are lacking vitality, let us wisely recall these words in order that we may regain it, for God is the Source of Life of all Creation, Who gives energy to the sun, all plants and animals, and all people.

We receive our needed renewal through the spiritual channels of our minds and the sacraments. Energy and strength will come to us and the only language we need for receiving it is prayer, wholehearted and true. We will experience help coming our way immediately, physically, spiritually, and mentally. The more we practice this, the stronger and better off we will be. It will bring us closer to God and to a life that is simple and real. Instead of feeling hopeless in the midst of many problems, good things, including the power to deal with them, will start coming our way. Only faith in God can renew all life!

October, 1960

THE POWER OF BELIEVING

It is common knowledge that the human body has the power to resist all sorts of diseases and to recover from many diseases to which it succumbs. Sometimes stories of such healing can be quite astonishing. Of course, there are many physiological reasons that account for this, but do we ever stop to consider the great power that is within us, the power of the mind and spirit that exceeds the power of our physical bodies? We read about this inner power in the pages of the Bible. It is our ability to imagine and be creative, to act justly toward others, to love God and neighbor, and, above all, to believe.

The quality of our life depends upon the extent to which we cultivate and develop this God-given faculty. Doing so enables us to overcome defeat in life. Indeed, the greatest issue of all times, and especially in our own times, is learning to believe.

One of the most important passages in all of Scripture is found in the Gospel according to St. Mark, where Jesus assures us that, "All things can be done for the one who believes" (Mark 9:23). But how and when is it to be done? First of all, we must place these words at the center of our minds and thought. If we do so, we can never be victims of a lowly spirit. The text does not mean that we will get everything we want, for our desire must follow the basic law of God's will. Then, the stronger our faith, the nearer we will come to success, reducing the impossible and vastly increasing the realm of possibility! Believe and practice believing, for spiritual power is immeasurable and can control our body and our life, directing it in the way that God wills for us to do. Only believe!

November, 1960

INNER JOY

Occasionally we meet someone who appears to be living a life of inner joy and happiness, one whose life recreates and radiates positive things all around. When we see such a person, we usually remark that he or she is enthusiastic. In truth, the very sense of the word "enthusiasm," in its Greek root, means "God within." Isn't it striking that the basic recipe for a joyous life is simply in finding God!

A physician once remarked that a large number of his patients did not require medicine so much as simply needing God. The wise have observed, "To know God is to live." But how is God to be found? God answers that question through the Prophet Jeremiah: "When you search for me you will find me, if you seek me with all your heart" (Jer. 29:13).

Say these words over and over until your mind comes naturally to accept the fact that God comes into our lives when we invite Him with all our being, opening the gates of our heart from the inside. He will not come uninvited. No one else can open the door for us, because the lock is on the inside. The moment you are willing to give over your whole self to God—surrendering your life, your loved ones, your health, your victories and defeats—He will come to you and help you in ways you never dreamed possible. God gives Himself to the profoundly sincere and the deeply desiring. It is said, "show me a man who truly knows God, and I will show you a happy, enthusiastic, and vital man."

February, 1961

LOVE ONE ANOTHER

In his letter to the Romans, St. Paul reminds us of the need for brotherly love with these words, " Love one another with mutual affection; outdo one another in showing honor" (Rom 12:10).

The status of our relations with other people has a remarkable effect on our spirits and minds. If we love others, a state of joy exists. We may compare that state with the words of a well-known writer who said, "The heart of him who truly loves is a paradise on earth; he has God in himself, for God is love."

The Lenten season is a time when we must practice this virtue. We must practice kindness and affection toward others. Above all, we must forgive others in order to free ourselves. We must be ready to demonstrate a generous and forbearing attitude and to assume that the difficult person we encounter is really a fine human being who is not truly as mean-spirited as he or she seems. Doing so elevates this kindness to affection, and from that to a level of love that puts the other person ahead of oneself. This is the supreme quality of courtesy, which has an amazing power to remove ill will, freeing our hearts from jealousy and malice and promoting all the best things in life.

The love we show toward others will give us in return great satisfaction. Our spirits will be lifted to new levels of happiness and joy.

March, 1961

FAITH, HOPE, AND LOVE

The key to immortality in the Christian life is found in this timeless statement of St. Paul, "And now faith, hope, and love abide, these three; and the greatest of these is love" (1 Cor 13:13).

The first of these, faith, includes faith in God and Christ, faith in oneself, and faith in others. Faith is the most effective power in the world and it can be ours. Someone once said of faith that it is "the pencil of the soul that pictures heavenly things."

Hope comes next. It is the attitude of expectancy, believing that the best is yet to come and that opportunity lies ahead. Believe this and it will be so. Hope, it has been said, proves man deathless. It is the struggle of the soul breaking loose from what is perishable and embracing eternity.

Finally, there is love, the greatest of the three. With love one's heart is emptied of hate, resentment, or ill will. Instead, the heart is filled with good will, compassion, understanding, and a desire to help others. Christian love offers a deep joy, for the heart of one who truly loves recreates a paradise on earth. God abides in that heart, for God is love.

Let us strive to make a suitable place in our heart, mind, and soul for these three supreme values.

June, 1961

THE DIVINELY ORDERED LIFE

An enjoyable life lived to the fullest is one that is well organized and governed by the law of God, the same law that orders the universe, nature and life itself. When we lack that ordering principle in our lives, we start to lose control over ourselves, falling prey to irritation, resentment, anxiety, and sinful activities.

Of course, no one in a right mind wants to be that way, but we end up in that state when we lack that inner spiritual force that allows us to exercise discipline over ourselves. Our problems overtake us and we begin losing the joy and freedom of a life governed by God; indeed, life itself begins to depart from us and the more frustrated we become.

It is never too late to begin exercising self-discipline and regaining control over lost things. When we submit ourselves to the will and guidance of God, we find ourselves on the way to a most pleasing victory over human weakness and sin. This is not an easy victory, but because it has to do with life itself, it is the only real victory worth striving to achieve. As Scripture says, "Those who conquer will inherit these things, and I will be their God and they will be my children" (Rev. 21:7).

This passage affirms that we will first have to realize and accept the fact that we are children of God. As a loving parent, God will be our help and our guide, so that instead of being overcome, we may overcome the adversities of life. Life then becomes meaningful and joyous as we find good things coming our way. It is then that we wholly understand the words of the Bible regarding our "inheritance," as in a most remarkable manner life in all its fullness starts coming our way.

July, 1961

FIGHTING THE GOOD FIGHT

We truly enjoy rest only after the accomplishment of real labor, for the fruit of labor is sweet. True joy in life depends upon the sincerity with which we apply ourselves to work in life and we find that we must struggle to keep the quality of our life at its best. Often we find ourselves called into real battle in order to defend the things we have been given. That is why in the Epistle to the Ephesians, St. Paul advises us to "take the shield of faith, with which you will be able to quench all the flaming arrows of the evil one. Take the helmet of salvation, and the sword of the Spirit, which is the word of God" (Eph. 6:16-17).

In olden days, when a man wore armor he carried a shield that protected his heart. For us, the shield that protects us is our faith in God. As the shield was relied upon to protect the physical heart, the center of our life, so too with faith do we protect the heart of our spiritual life from any sort of attack by what St. Paul calls the "fiery darts of the evil one." Indeed, those darts are many and the only way to quench them is to be armed with faith.

St. Paul also refers to the helmet of salvation. As the knight always protected his head, so too must we protect our mind from the many damaging attitudes that erode its effectiveness: fear, hate, evil thoughts, jealousy, greed, and so on. First, the mind must be kept clean and continually refilled with good things, that is, things that promote and radiate life.

In addition to protecting our heart and mind, the Apostle advises us to arm ourselves with the sword of God's word by which we may overcome the enemies of our inner peace and life, namely, wrong thinking and wrongdoing. We must never lower our guard after a single victory, for battles may be won along the way, but the war is a lifelong one. We must always be on our guard and armed with the sword of God's word, if we want to enjoy the days of our life. Our hearts must be allowed to remain the source of faith, hope, and love. And our minds must be free to enjoy the best that life has to offer, centered by God's word through constant prayer.

August, 1961

ON OVERCOMING FEAR (Part I)

It is often said that we are what we think, say, or do. Perhaps becoming what we think is where the problem starts, for this is what happens (or should happen!) first in our lives. In the biblical story of Job we find these words: "Truly the thing that I fear comes upon me, and what I dread befalls me" (Job 3:25).

This is a very serious warning for us. If, over a long period of time, a person habitually fears something, there is a tendency for that fear to become a reality and the matter becomes a self-fulfilling prophecy. For example, if one fears that he or she is going to fall, so that the thought of falling is constantly entertained, a mental condition is likely to come about that may even produce the fall. If the mind is filled with defeatist attitudes, defeat will surely come our way.

Since what it is we put in our minds tends to govern our direction, then why not put faith in God as our first principle of thought? This way we give over our will and our lives to the care of God, the highest and best purpose in the world, enveloping ourselves in an atmosphere of hope that illuminates even the darkest hours. This spiritual direction will surely lead us to success, better health, and well being.

Someone once said that good men have the fewest fears and he that fears doing wrong has only one. Wrong deeds must be corrected, sins repented, and fears forgotten for beginning the new life in Christ. As St. Paul writes, ". . . this one thing I do: forgetting what lies behind and straining forward to what lies ahead, I press on toward the goal for the prize of the heavenly call of God in Christ Jesus" (Phil 3:13-14). Only in company with God can we look with confidence toward the future.

October, 1961

OVERCOMING FEAR (Part II)

The further we move away from God, the closer we move toward Fear. When we first start becoming insecure in our lives, the insecurity begins spreading until it pervades and dominates every aspect of our being. We start looking for remedies outside ourselves, ways to compensate for, mask, and escape those growing fears.

The Bible urges us to call upon God for help in fearful times. Psalm 27:1, for example, proclaims, "The Lord is my light and my salvation; whom shall I fear? The Lord is the stronghold of my life; of whom shall I be afraid?"

The moment we are willing to surrender our whole life to God, including our loved ones, our business, our own health and well being, we are immediately granted peace and begin experiencing help that we never before dreamed possible. God gives Himself to the profoundly sincere and the deeply desiring, so if we wish to overcome fear, simply remember Psalm 27, calling upon God to remove all fear. In its place you will receive life, with joy as its reward.

March, 1964

ON CONFESSION

The practice of Confession in the Orthodox Church was instituted in order that we may remain spiritually awake and alive. Often, one of the reasons we hesitate or refuse to confess our sins is that we still remain in them. When we come to the point where we feel the need or desire to confess our evil thoughts and deeds, it shows that we are finally waking up to our truer self. It is like a person waking up from a terrible dream and feeling the need to talk about it in order to lessen its power.

We are advised not to be ashamed at confessing our wrongs, for in so doing we demonstrate the true self-awareness necessary to begin correcting the error of our ways. St. James advises us to "confess your sins to one another, and pray for one another, so that you may be healed. The prayer of the righteous is powerful and effective" (James 5:16).

When physically sick, we see a doctor in order to receive help in overcoming our illness. Seldom do we think of the true causes of our sickness, and the extent to which it is fed through buried resentments and burdens of guilt. With confession and repentance we rid ourselves of these poisons, cleansing our mind and soul so that the poison does not infiltrate the body. The technique involves confessing our faults, engaging in prayer, and truly believing that God can empower us to overcome the things that cause us to stumble. Only confession opens the channel of God's mercy to flow our way. If we do not have a repentant mind and heart, God's mercy can never be ours to enjoy. For without God's mercy, there can be no life.

November, 1961

HOW A WORD OF GOD CAN HELP US

With the words "Let us attend! Let us listen to the wisdom of the Holy Gospel," proclaimed at every Divine Liturgy, the priest or deacon calls our attention to that very important aspect of our worship, the portion of the Gospel assigned by the Church for that day. For the multitude of Orthodox believers across the world who stand and hear the Gospel alongside us, the Bible provides supernatural strength and power.

The Bible is written in simple language that everyone can understand. As our everyday problems increase, our understanding of the Bible may increase as well. Unfortunately, however, the majority of people prefer to complain about the ills in our lives, rather than seek the promise of a remedy.

Often when we are in trouble we seek a close trusted friend who can help us. But the closest and most trusted friend of all is God. When we are afflicted by our moods, feeling worried, fearful, angry, resentful, or lonely, there is always an answer in the Bible. So if you have a Bible lying around, perhaps one of sentimental value that was given to you by your parents, priest, or Sunday School teacher, take it and read it. You will find consolation and good counsel in its pages. You may pray to have God direct you to the passage you need. The first passage you open to may not speak to you, for God does not necessarily work in such a mechanically predictable way, but keep reading and you will come to what it is God desires to have you hear. You will recognize it when you see it. With time you will become more and more familiar with the Bible and be able to recall which passages help in specific situations.

It is suggested that we read through the Gospels first: Matthew, Mark, Luke, and John, the first four books of the New Testament. Try reading at least a chapter each day. Some people enjoy reading in the morning, but I personally recommend reading your daily chapter each night upon retiring. This will allow you to sleep with the healthiest, happiest, and most positive thoughts possible, soaking into your being in preparation for the following day. By your second or third reading, try to begin memorizing a passage or two. This way the Gospels will become a permanent part of your being. The more passages you commit to memory, the more equipped your mind will be in bringing the Bible to your aid, for the Gospels show us the principles of Christ's life. If we master them, we learn His rare secret for great living.

Therefore do not miss a day in heeding the call to "attend and listen to the wisdom of the Holy Gospel." Remember those words so that you may always find help, good counsel, guidance, and healing, whenever the need next arises.

June, 1962

BELONGING TO THE CHURCH

Why do we belong to the Church? Is it because others belong, or because it appears to be rich in property and possessions? Does belonging to the Church carry the promise of enhancing our influence in the community? All of these aspects may be served, but none of them should be the primary reason for belonging. We belong to the Church because of Christ her founder, and because of the Gospel.

Christ Jesus fed many thousands, but He was followed by only twelve close followers, one of which later betrayed Him. He had no worldly possessions to speak of, and even the garment He wore was gambled away by the Roman soldiers who mocked Him on the way to the Cross. Roman authority was the dominant influence of Christ's day, and our Savior wrote not even a single book, but through His teaching and the example of His life He prevails in the world today. Americans of Serbian descent have been entrusted with the responsibility of furthering the Gospel through the ministry of our Church, expanding the Kingdom of God on earth through our local community.

We may fail in this God-given responsibility, but we cannot expect others to succeed for us. We may compare and compete only with ourselves, taking our yesterday fully into today and looking forward into tomorrow. Will we find when it is too late that we could have done so much better? Most of us share the conviction that our church community should become more dynamic and prosperous, so let us look around to see what may be missing and where improvement might occur.

July, 1962

ON RENEWAL

Our inner life has a lot in common with the nature that surrounds us. The human spirit is like the good earth, which must experience times of renewal and replenishment. Everyday life adds layer upon layer of dust on our souls. As a result, our inner life can become barren and bleak, like the dry earth that from valley to mountain awaits the thunder, lightning, and strong winds that carry the comforting promise of refreshment through rain.

This thought reminds us of a verse from the Bible. "Repent, therefore, and turn to God so that your sins may be wiped out, so that times of refreshing may come from the presence of the Lord . . ." (Acts 3:19-20). Through wrong thinking and wrongdoing the freshness of our mind and soul quickly fades and we become suffocated by the dust of sin, making us barren and dead. When we truly repent, we are restored to our original freshness and vitality. Someone once said that repentance is a hearty sorrow over our past misdeeds and a sincere resolution and endeavor to live our lives in conformity with the law of God. Repentance does not consist in the single act of sorrow, but in performing deeds of repentance for the remainder of our lives in sincere obedience to Christ our Lord. Our inner life will be renewed, our soul refreshed like the day following a cleansing, powerful rain.

November, 1962

"...AND RENEW A RIGHT SPIRIT WITHIN ME"

Often we feel that life has become too tedious, too mundane, loaded with worries that carry over from day to day, sometimes bringing us to the point where we feel as though we can no longer bear our burdens. We forget the words of Christ our Savior, who urged us, saying, "Come to me, all you that are weary and are carrying heavy burdens, and I will give you rest" (Matt 11:28). And of course the burdens here are not the physical kind that strain and bruise our muscles, but the burdens of life that weigh heavily on our heart and mind.

Christ's words in this verse provide a spiritual pain reliever for this kind of ailment. It is a medicine that should be taken often. How does it work? By showing us the proper way—Christ's way of thinking and doing.

"Learn of me," He says. In other words, work by His method. "My yoke is easy, and my burden light," so that with Him "all things are possible." Suddenly life becomes a joy, even in the midst of adversity. We will come to have new friends, better health, more happiness and increased success. Following the way of Christ will help us shed our irritability, selfishness, and arrogance that threaten our relationship towards other people and towards God. When our spirit is renewed, we find ourselves accepted by others and have a better sense of being accepted by God. So let no day pass without saying, "Renew a right spirit within me," so that God can act to restore us to peace and strength in our homes, at work, and in our Church.

February, 1964

SPIRITUAL HEALING

Did you know that we could call upon God to heal us of all infirmities caused by spiritual depression? Many physical and emotional difficulties arise from this unfortunate condition, but He can restore us to completeness, healing all the scars and abrasions of our soul. Just as Christ was a physician for those in need in New Testament times, so now may we still seek Him for the remedy against our emotional and physical disturbances:

> And wherever he went, into villages or cities or farms, they laid the sick in the marketplaces, and begged him that they might touch even the fringe of his cloak; and all who touched it were healed" (Mark 6:56).

Participating in the life of the Church we are reminded to keep our mind occupied with thoughts of God as we actively follow the teachings of Christ, consistently practicing a mental attitude of trust that rewards us with a strange and wonderful experience of being watched over, protected, and guided. There will be so much evidence for this fact that no doubt can remain that everlasting goodness hovers above, for as the Bible reminds us, "For he will command his angels concerning you to guard you in all your ways" (Psalm 91:11).

Take this promise to heart and see how your spirit will rise, knowing there is nothing in the world that can harm us—neither pain, nor hardship, nor even death itself—for God watches over us all. He has given us His Holy Church, which is governed by His Spirit, to guide you in safety and in peace. May God protect and love you all.

July, 1964

ON TEMPTATION

Temptations of various sorts assail us always. The Bible tells us that even Christ was tempted, just as we are, but Christ withstood temptation and prevailed against it. We demonstrate and increase our strength each time we are able to resist temptation, but giving in almost always results in feelings of failure and loss of self-respect.

These defeats tend to dull the spirit, robbing us of the heightened sense of happiness and well-being one enjoys when practicing self-discipline. Yielding repeatedly to the same temptation eventually depletes the joy of living.

No matter how much we are tempted, or how low our spirit has been brought down, we are called upon to mobilize all our resources in the continued struggle to do our best. The Bible offers us a resource to that end:

> No testing has overtaken you that is not common to everyone. God is faithful, and he will not let you be tested beyond your strength, but with the testing he will also provide the way out so that you may be able to endure it. (1 Cor. 10:13)

With faith in God we need never suffer moral defeat, for with every temptation comes a way with God to overcome it. A sincere desire for God's help is all that is needed, asking and believing that He will abide with us through difficult times. With each victory we will experience increased joy and a rehabilitation of our self-respect. Let us pray that God grants us the wisdom to call upon Him the next moment temptation rises up before us.

December, 1964

OUR TRUE POTENTIAL

The Parable of the Talents (Matt. 25:14-30) impresses upon us the importance of putting to good use the gifts God has entrusted to us. Each of us differs in the kind of gifts we possess, but faithfulness in the consecration and dedication of these gifts in the performance of our duty is demanded equally of us all. Here the quality of our character is put to the test. When we meet the challenge successfully, we qualify ourselves for greater responsibility. Created in the image and likeness of God, human beings are called upon to create good, including truth, justice, love, and strength of character, beauty, and harmony.

The psychology of modern living amply demonstrates that unused physical, mental, and moral capacity takes a toll upon life, diminishing it and threatening its very existence. Christ warns us that gifts that are not put to use will be taken away from us, thus the complacency that characterizes so many of our Churches today must be abandoned. Let us make every effort to keep our prayer before God to sustain us in this work.

October, 1965

THE GOOD SAMARITAN

In the Parable of the Good Samaritan (Luke 10:25-37), Jesus presents an illustration of the greatest commandment of all, the twofold obligation to love God and love one another. This commandment is the cornerstone of the Christian faith, for Jesus incorporated this principle into His very life. Genuine love of God includes true reverence and awe, while love for human beings comprises admiration, respect, and a desire to offer aid and comfort. This is what it means to be created in the image and likeness of God, for here the faculties of our personality are integrated. We possess a genuine desire to acquire the spirit of God and be of service in the fulfillment of the Divine Will.

As love generates life, the offering of compassion nourishes and preserves life in the midst of a world of violence and hostility. But the question arises, "Who is my neighbor?" As the parable indicates, it was not a man of rank and position, as a scribe or priest, who came to the aid of his victimized countryman, but a Samaritan. From the perspective of many Jews living during the time of Jesus, Samaritans were considered to be somewhat less than second-class citizens. Yet it was this lowly stranger who had compassion on the victim and demonstrated what it truly means to be one's neighbor.

Christ Himself becomes as the Samaritan, for this was His mission in the world, proving himself our true Neighbor at such great cost. It is now up to us to prove ourselves as neighbors in a

Words of a Shepherd

hostile world, for we are called to love for God and fellow human beings for the life of the world.

December, 1965

INVITED GUESTS

Through prayer our soul is able to penetrate the dense fog of fear and sin that obscures our view of God. Prayer unites us with the Spirit of God, recreating and restoring us through grace to new life. It breaks down the walls that isolate us and keep us separated from God and our fellow human beings. The walls, which are constructed by sins of pride and foolishness, imprison us, stifling our creativity and suffocating our spirit.

Prayer brings us out of our exile in the wilderness and leads us to the threshold of everlasting joy and love. There our Heavenly Host invites us in as guests, sharing bread and salt, the customary sign of welcome and acceptance. Sharing this symbolic meal we become close friends with Him, obligated to loyalty and faith. Jesus reminds us of the fact that we must be good hosts, gladly receiving those who come to our door. How much more our Heavenly Father delights in greeting us and welcoming us through the open doors of joy, love, and grace. Let me illustrate this point further: Suppose the billions of human beings living on our planet were suddenly able to bring together all their good will and love and welcome us into their fold. What a splendid embrace that would be! But God is so much more than that! And we remain forever his welcomed precious guests. Why not, then, put an end to our lonely isolation? Simply knock on the door and ask.

Whenever we separate ourselves from God and one another, we repeat Adam's sin, for the first human also wanted to hide, separated from God by his sin. Does this story really need to be repeated again in this world? The arms of eternal life, creation, and joy extend toward you and me. Shall we accept them in faith and prayer?

December, 1966

IN THE IMAGE AND LIKENESS OF GOD

It is important for us to remember that we are created in the image and likeness of God (Gen. 1:27). Our love for truth, beauty, harmony, charity, and justice, of life and things imperishable, all of these evidence the image of God in us. This image can be blurred and obscured, but it can never be completely destroyed. The highest and best fulfillment of the image is revealed through our creative work as Christians in a Church whose head is Christ.

A true Christian life will mirror the life of Christ. For us, living such a life calls for constant effort. It involves strengthening the bonds of mutual love for one another and avoiding the negative behaviors of faultfinding and denigration that destroy the image of God in us. This kind of action results in spiritual death. "Repent, therefore, and be converted, that your sins may be blotted out, when the times of refreshing shall come from the presence of the Lord" (Acts 3:19).

As the earth suffers periods of drought lasting months or even years at a time, so too does our inner life sometimes become arid and covered with dust, barren and dead. Through personal and sincere repentance we prepare ourselves for the refreshing waters of God's grace. His image in us is restored and we are renewed.

Let us pray to God for prudence and strength, that we may always be on our guard spiritually, bearing His image and likeness through living a Christ-like life in our homes, in our Church,, and in society.

February, 1966

SUFFERING

Most of us would certainly enjoy a life of constant joy, free of all suffering. Some of the greatest minds stumble on this point and rebel against Christ, for they cannot understand the meaning of suffering. First, one must understand the meaning of joy. Joy is the greatest triumph of life; it is the symbol of creative work. Because the redemptive work of Christ was the greatest work ever wrought, the joy of Christ is supreme.

The suffering of Christ affords St. Paul an opportunity to address the sufferings of Christians in his day, urging them to "take Christ as your example." We should also remember the words in the Book of Proverbs, where suffering is described as the Lord's discipline. God disciplines whom He loves and scourges everyone upon whom He bestows the name of son. It is, therefore, for the sake of discipline that one must endure sufferings. God is treating us as His children, and discipline is a necessary element in this type of relationship. God's discipline is perfect. The end He has in view is to make us partakers of His own Holiness.

To most of us, discipline often seems painful and irksome at the time, but divine discipline ultimately produces a life of peace and righteousness. When we are ready to rebel and reject the situation in which we find ourselves, let us exercise patience and prayer, for it is this that opens the doors of hope and wisdom. Christ showed us an example in this way, establishing His

Church in order to teach us to become Christ-like, and therefore God-like. The greater our suffering, the closer to God we become.

June, 1966

ON THE PARABLE OF THE WEDDING FEAST

(Matt. 22:1-14; Luke 14:16-24)

The main point of this parable is to teach us that those for whom the Kingdom of God is intended can lose their privileges because they did not value them. In this case, the privileges were given to the despised outsider. This story stresses the truth that God's purpose is never thwarted by human beings, for guests can always be found to attend the banquet of the King.

The broad universal note of the Gospel rings clearly here. Note the kind of excuses each invited guest gives. They are the normal, everyday concerns of life, things not sinful in themselves, but which often absorb all of our thoughts and energies and stand between us and full acceptance of the joy in partaking in God's Kingdom. Comparing the Kingdom of God to a wedding feast serves to emphasize the joy and celebration of life in the God's Kingdom.

"I have purchased a plot of land and I must go see it. . ." is the excuse of those for whom the concerns of this world are in the forefront, distracting us from unseen spiritual realities.

"I have purchased five yoke of oxen and I must go to prove them…" say those who prefer the ways and means of obtaining the riches of this world, ignoring the treasure in Heaven.

"I have married a wife and therefore cannot come. . ." is the excuse of those who put loyalty to human beings above loyalty to God and His Kingdom.

God calls us to freedom and joy, but human beings often choose slavery to the things of this world and thus reject God. The peoples' rejection of God leads to God's rejection of the people. The invitation is extended to the man on the street. "But I have no wedding garment," he says. Indeed, even he cannot come to the feast, emphasizing the fact that one must appear at the royal banquet with the pure garment of righteousness and that the day will come when the King of Righteousness will come to sift the worthy from the unworthy. Such a note of divine severity appears often in the teachings of our Lord Jesus Christ. We would do well to heed such messages.

September, 1966

OUR INNER VOICE

Whenever we find ourselves confronted by the need to choose some moral action, something that happens quite often during the course of the day, we are called upon to hearken to that inner voice inside us. Often our will struggles within us, but that voice within us informs us of the right choice even though we may choose to ignore it, attesting to the spirit of God and right reason in every soul. This ability enables us to live our lives in well-being through the perils of temptations to things that ultimately harm us, destroying inner peace and alienating us from God. As long as we are willing to listen to that inner voice and act accordingly our lives will radiate with the glow of energy, life, and hope.

As Orthodox Christians, we carry the conviction that no theory of living found in any book except the Bible, nor by any person except Christ, can help us become more attuned to the practice of listening to that inner voice. No matter how great the temptation, God gives us the strength to overcome it. The greater the temptation we overcome, the greater our sense of victory and assurance that the Kingdom of God is within us, filling us with confidence and joy and abundant spiritual energy. As God's word assures us, "I will dwell in them and walk in them; and I will be their God and they shall be My people."

February, 1967

OUTWARD SIGNS OF OUR FAITH

It is important for us to know about some of the outward symbols we use in our worship, signs that express our inner prayers. Quietly folded hands and bowed heads are ways that we participate with our bodies in prayer and acknowledge God's sovereign power over all creation. The Church is the place where our prayers are brought and offered up. Our prayers are on our lips when we enter the Church, as all other kinds of talking cease. As we light our candle, a symbol of our prayer, and take our places, we do so quietly and on tiptoe, mindful of others in maintaining the prayerful atmosphere of God's house.

The hymns of praise and words of prayer that arise to the throne of God in Heaven as sweet incense from the hearts of His children, are they not pleasing to our Heavenly Father? Just ask the human father whether or not he treasures the care of his children as they run with outstretched arms into his loving embrace at the end of the day's work. Ask him if the light of love that glows in their eyes and the tender play of those angelic hands on the wrinkles of his work-worn countenance are meaningless and empty. Are they not the food for his heart and the very breath of his being?

God has not created His children to be set adrift in life's ocean, without care for their happiness and well-being. He has fashioned their hearts after the likeness of His own, giving His children the ability to communicate with Him and come to Him with their needs and their love.

God's parental heart rejoices at the outpourings of His children's love and praise; it is saddened by their indifference and neglect. That is why the performance of external acts of adoration and praise constitute the greater part of our worship service. St. John reminds us that God is due "all benediction and glory, wisdom, thanksgiving, honor, and power forever and ever" (1 John 7:12).

Finally, we should take this opportunity to call to mind the icons in our Church, Saints whose exemplary lives participate with ours in offering up praise to our Heavenly Father. We gaze upon that rich treasury of our tradition of icons and find the support we need. Let us remain mindful and observant of all of these outward signs of our faith.

July, 1968

TWO WAYS

In the Bible we read that there are two paths in life: the way of God and the way of men. How can we know which is the way of God? By remembering that we are created in the image of God, which means a mind and free will that can be guided by the spirit of God within us. If we make proper use of this faculty, then we may progress toward the goal of eternal life in Him. For this reason Christ tells us, "You, therefore, must be perfect." Furthermore, St. Paul admonishes us, "Be not conformed to this world, but be transformed by the renewing of your mind, that you may prove what is that good, acceptable, and perfect will of God" (Rom. 12:2).

It is up to us to choose whether we will follow the will of God or the way of the world, which is to follow our own will. One of the most difficult things in life is having to deal with the need for constant choosing even of things that are mundane. We must remember that Christ, too, was confronted by choices. In the desert he was confronted by the temptation of choosing to turn stones into bread that he might eat, but he chose instead to continue doing the will of His Father in Heaven, even unto death on the Cross. Christ chose suffering in order to rescue and preserve the dignity of man, the image of God in us. To understand life in the world any other way is spiritual blindness.

Jesus Christ shows us that self-will opposes the way of God, leading us into malice, envy, bitterness, malcontent, impatience, and numerous dark passions that reign in the hearts of the wicked. Our Lord directs us with these words, "After this manner pray: Our Father who art in Heaven, hallowed be Thy Name. Thy Kingdom come; Thy Will be done on earth as it is in Heaven. . ." (Matt. 6:9-11).

June, 1969

ON THE HOLY SPIRIT

It is the Spirit of God who enters the world and gives it movement and life, breaking into human history and giving mankind its sense of its existence. Before the start of each Holy Liturgy the priest recites the prayer to the Holy Spirit, "O Heavenly King, the Comforter and Spirit of Truth, Who art everywhere and fillest all things, Treasury of blessing and Giver of Life, come and abide in us and cleanse us from every impurity and save our souls, O Good One." Just as the Holy Spirit enlightened and strengthened the Apostles on the first Pentecost, each of us receives Him at the time of our Baptism and Chrismation. Stir up within yourself the grace of the Holy Spirit given to you then, and honor the Holy Spirit, God, today.

THE HOLY SCRIPTURES

The Holy Bible is the Church's book. The writings contained in it, called the canon, were collected by early Christian leaders operating under the guidance of the Holy Spirit. There were many other writings circulating at the time, but if a particular text was widely read, tied to an Apostle, and resonated with truth as led by the Holy Spirit, it was given the Church's seal of approval as an inspired text.

The Scriptures play a profound role in the life and work of the Orthodox Church. The Psalms make up the Church's prayerbook; the Gospels are highly revered and placed in the center of the altar; lessons from the epistles are read at every liturgy; and the fabric of the liturgy itself is biblical, heard in such facets as the Prokeimenon, which is heard just before the Gospel reading.

Who is the author of Scripture? Ultimately, the Church affirms, it is God. Of course, the words were written down and copied by scribes, perhaps more than forty all together, but these were writers inspired and illumined by the Holy Spirit. God inspired men from all walks of life in the writing of His book. Some were poets, philosophers, fishermen, statesmen, prophets, physicians, exiles, tax collectors, judges, shepherds, and many others.

The writings of the Bible were composed in a variety of places and over a long period of time. The books of the Old Testament were written almost entirely in Hebrew. Sometime during the third century B.C., the Hebrew Bible was translated into

Greek, the lingua franca of the time, for Jews living outside of Palestine. Greek was also the language in which the books of the New Testament were originally composed, except for a few phrases in Aramaic, the language spoken by Jesus. The Bible is now the most translated book in the world, published in thousands of languages.

There are no surviving original manuscripts of the Bible. We do not have the scrolls upon which Moses, Isaiah, Mark, or Paul wrote, but we have several ancient copies of these originals. Some years ago, in 1948, considerable excitement was created when a Bedouin shepherd boy found some ancient sealed jars in a cave near the Dead Sea. In the jars were found seven ancient parchment scrolls that had been preserved for nearly two thousand years in the arid climate of the Judean desert. Over the next decade, other scrolls were found in nearby caves, yielding copies of every book of the Old Testament (except Esther). Prior to the discovery, the oldest existing manuscripts of the Old Testament went back only about a thousand years. With the finding of the Dead Sea Scrolls, we now possess manuscripts that go back to the time of Christ. Scholars were amazed to find that the tradition of copying manuscripts had remained carefully accurate all those centuries, giving us the assurance that the Bible we read today is essentially the Bible as it was written so many centuries ago.

What is the subject matter contained in God's Word? The topics are as varied as the men whom God used to write them. The Bible contains history, law, genealogy, prophecy, poetry, music, dietary and purity codes, and several other genres. All of these have a special purpose, uniting to reveal God's plan of salvation for mankind. St. John summed it all up in his gospel when he wrote, "These [words] were written that you might believe that Jesus is the Christ, the Son of God, and that believing, you might have life through His name. . ."

And so it is that the Orthodox Church reverences God's book, called the Word of God, for it contains His message to us in all times, in all places, in all of life's circumstances.

November, 1971

ATTENDING CHURCH

An intelligent businessman who would normally deny being a renegade excused himself for never going to Church except on Christmas and Easter, with the excuse that when he was a boy, the priest required that he attend Church every Sunday so that he had "more than his share of Church-going at that time." A female colleague of his said, "I'm a better Christian than lots of people who never miss Church, but in the summer I take a vacation from Church-going." We hear this a lot, but think about how silly it is. Let's think of it this way. Imagine a man refuses to bathe on the grounds that as a child he had been bathed enough, or a woman who declines to style her hair in the summer because she needs a vacation from it.

Going to Church is not the whole of Christianity. Conversely, it is possible to attend Church regularly and still be a villainous hypocrite. Still, it remains true that the Christian religion requires certain duties of its adherents, including the hallowing of the Lord's day by regular attendance in worship at the Lord's house. One's personal preferences cannot preclude this; it is a sacred obligation.

Other excuses abound. The music is wretched! The preacher is stupid! The service is too ornate, or too plain. The congregation is too large, or too small. People do not speak to me! Even if these statements were accurate, it does not affect one's duty.

To an atheist or agnostic, all of this means nothing. If there is no God, then one is not bound to keep His commandments. But what of the man who is baptized and calls himself a Christian, expecting the blessings of the Church on his marriage and eventual burial, outwardly honoring the Word of God, yet despising one of the plainest of God's commandments, observing it only when he feels like it? We must realize that failing to attend Church regularly carries grave import for the well-being of our souls.

October, 1971

TESTING YOUR KNOWLEDGE

Each state requires that a driver first undergo an examination of his or her ability to operate a motor vehicle before obtaining a license to drive. This is done not only for the protection of other people, but to safeguard the life of the driver as well.

We are charged with the responsibility of operating our own life and its destiny, a charge which comes from God, our Creator. How well we meet that challenge will not only determine the kind of life we have in this world, but on the other side of death as well. It will also influence those around us, especially our family and friends. A person's life reflects the precepts one believes in. This is especially telling for Orthodox Christians, who are called to live a Christ-centered life. For that reason it would be to our advantage to take the time to see how much we know about our faith, what it stands for, what is expected of us, and the ways we benefit from knowing it and living its precepts. Superficial knowledge would not be enough in this respect, just as a lack of knowledge would not allow a driver to obtain a license to drive a car on the streets.

The knowledge we need to open the channels of grace comes from our participation in the life of the Church, especially by attending the Divine Liturgy. We need to exert the effort, to study and learn how to live out our faith and do the things we claim to believe. Only then can we endure when tested by the fires of life.

April, 1972

GODPARENTHOOD

Sooner or later, most Orthodox Christians are asked to be sponsors at the Baptism and Chrismation of a newborn or convert to the Church. Therefore we ought to be interested enough in this matter to know what is involved in this ancient practice.

First of all, it is an honor to be asked to be a godparent, but one should be aware that acceptance of this request imposes responsibilities that last a lifetime. Our Lord called Baptism a second birth. So just as a child is born naturally of a father and mother, so, too, is one born spiritually through this sacrament, having spiritual parents or sponsors.

Just as natural parents have serious obligations for the care and nurture of their child, so, too, do godparents have important duties in respect to their godchild, especially in regard to seeing that he or she receives a Christian upbringing. This means that the sponsors are not to forget their godchildren after the Church ceremonies, or that all they have to do is send a card or gift on birthdays. How much better it would be if godparents remembered their godchildren on spiritual birthdays, the date of their Baptism and Chrismation, giving them some gift of religious significance, like an icon or prayerbook, Bible or cross! Even more so, imagine how glorious it would be if they gathered with the family to observe these spiritual anniversaries.

Surely being a godparent brings the responsibility of praying for the godchild. How often do sponsors pray for their spiritual children? How often do they remember them during the

Divine Liturgy, asking God to bless the child they brought into the Church for the very first time. Care and concern, prayer and petition are the ingredients that go into a sponsor's duties. If, by chance, the parents themselves neglect the spiritual nurture and Christian education of their child, surely it behooves the godparents to bring every effort to bear in dealing with the situation.

It is obvious from all of this that godparents themselves must be baptized and chrismated and members in good standing in their Orthodox communities. They must know and live their faith. It is the duty of the parents to choose their children's sponsors with care and deliberation. And it is the responsibility of the godparents to bring their godchildren to Christ.

June, 1972

THE TRUE LIGHT

Our Lord proclaimed, "I am the Light of the world. He who follows Me shall not walk in darkness, but shall have the light of life."

Many of us make a mistake in life by accepting the glare of the world instead of the true light that keeps us from darkness and despair. The glare blinds us from seeing our neighbor who is in need. It blinds us from God and His will for our life.

If we are to regain our true sight, to see the meaning and purpose that brings joy to life, a transformation must take place. We must come to Christ and ask Him, prayerfully and with faith, to open the eyes of our soul and spirit as he opened the eyes of the two blind men. With this miracle we, too, will begin to see. We will come to realize that without Jesus Christ no one can truly see, and with Him no one need remain blind.

February, 1973

OUR RESPONSIBILITIES

In order to answer the question "What does it mean to belong to the Church?" we must first know something about the nature of the Church. Here we must distinguish two elements. On the one hand, there is the divine aspect, unchanging God and the Spirit of Truth and Love. On the other hand, there is the human aspect, in all of its potentiality, and therefore change. For this reason Christ tells us, "Be ye perfect as my Father in Heaven is perfect." Therefore the Church is understood to be the place where, through prayer, fasting, constant moderation in every domain of life and work, we may become perfected in goodness and fit citizens of the Kingdom of God.

We become members of the Body of Christ that is, the Church at our baptism. This is something quite apart from paying membership dues in order to enjoy certain privileges in the Church. Our baptism must be constantly confirmed in affirming our faith in Christ and rejecting evil. The sacrament of Baptism must continually be confirmed in everyday life, making our choice for God.

A second important ingredient is prayer, especially that which is recited in the Divine Liturgy by those who prepare themselves for Holy Communion. When prayer is lacking in the life of the Church, then things like disrupting gossip begin to take place. The local Church by-laws state that one of the requirements for being a member in good standing is to prepare oneself for Holy Communion, taking the Sacrament during the Lenten season. Christ tells us, "Take, eat, this is my body . . ." and, "Drink ye all of this, for this is my blood of the New Testament. . ." This is the very center of our Liturgy and our faith. Without this, all becomes empty.

Another important ingredient of our responsibility is our work and our financial support. What sort of work? Each of us has certain skills and abilities that may benefit the Church. How much should I give? This question, too, must be answered individually. Whatever we possess, let us remember that it is already a gift from God to us. By sharing part of it in return, we acknowledge and give thanks for what we have.

The fourth component of our life in the Church is that we accept the discipline of the Church, to take upon ourselves the responsibility of accepting and guarding the order of the house of prayer, to support those entrusted with the responsibility of guiding it, including accepting and respecting the priestly order and higher Church authorities, for they are empowered through the Holy Spirit to do the work.

If the ingredients here are practiced only in part or not at all, the church eventually degenerates into nothing more than a social club named for a saint. Discouragement sets in, tensions grow, and the end is not far away.

June, 1973

REPETITION

Perhaps you have heard somebody say something like this: "I don't attend the Liturgy because I hear the same words over and over again. It's like going to a movie I've seen many times before. It's boring!"

In many cases, statements like this are simply an excuse for laziness in an effort to avoid personal responsibility. In addition, those who lack an understanding of the true nature of prayer and the power of religious symbolism blind themselves to the needs of the soul and spirit. These are the people who become bored. But consider that we eat, bathe, breathe, and engage in many other activities on a daily basis, performing each in the same way every day. Also, we sin and neglect God daily. Therefore it is only natural that we stand and say again and again, "Lord have mercy!"

July, 1973

REMEMBERING WHO WE ARE

As Orthodox Christians we are called upon to remember that our Church maintains a living connection with the patriarchs and prophets of the Old Testament, as well as the Apostles, martyrs, confessors, and teachers of our Church from the beginning until this day. This living interconnection is reenacted every Sunday in the service of Proskomede, or Office of Oblation. This demonstrates that we are not a recently founded religious community, neither was our Church established in the Middle Ages. The Orthodox Church was called "Orthodox," or "right belief," because of the great emphasis the early Fathers of the Church placed upon preserving the original faith.

The history of the Church is a living tradition in the life of the contemporary Church. The Holy Bible is the foundation of that tradition and is not considered separate from the life of the Church. It was the early Church that brought together the writings of the Bible; together with the ongoing prayer of the Church, these make up the elements of our sacred tradition.

There is a great sense of community in the Orthodox tradition. Orthodox Christians never pray alone, but with all the saints who have gone on before us. We do not pray as individuals, but as members of the body of Christ, that is, the Church. Together with the patriarchs and prophets, saints, martyrs and confessors, the Blessed Theotokos, Apostles and even angels, we pray. They stand with us in prayer at every liturgy, made present by the Holy

Icons. Gathered around the icon of Christ, they represent the Church triumphant, while we, gathered together on the floor of the Church, represent the Church militant on earth. Thus, around Christ both Heaven and Earth are united in celebration of the Name of our Lord.

The great physicist Albert Einstein once said, "A hundred times every day I remind myself that my inner and outer life depend on the labors of other men, living and dead. I must exert myself in order to give in the measure as I have received and am still receiving."

As Christians, we are "torch bearers." We have received the light of life from its source in God. The torch was handed to us by a great line of believers stretching all the way back to Christ. It is our duty and privilege to pass it on to others.

September, 1973

THE REAL KINGDOM

The Church instructs us to focus our attention on ourselves in order to become the kind of person God intends us to be. In that sense we are called to be a kind of ruler over ourselves. According to the Bible, every person is called to exercise princely authority over the earth, for God commands us to "replenish the earth and subdue it, and have dominion over the fish of the sea and over the fowl of the air, and over every living thing that moves upon the earth" (Gen. 1:28). Indeed, it seems that through science and technology mankind has indeed become master over the earth, even reaching for outer space. But in spite of all of this, mankind seems to be losing control over itself, the most immediate focus of our dominion. Alexander the Great is reported to have cried over having no more lands to conquer, but he lost control over himself and fell victim to alcohol and an early death.

Today human beings have conquered the natural world and rule over it with confidence. They control certain aspects of nature but cannot control their own tongues. They build huge dams that hold back millions of gallons of water, but remain slaves to alcohol, drugs, or sex. Man controls the power of the atom, but cannot command the respect of his own children or overcome his own appetites. Someone once said, "I have more trouble with myself than with anyone else I have ever known." Don't these words apply to us all?

81

Being a good and effective ruler over ourselves requires discipline, restraint, and self-denial. Outstanding minds of all ages have advised people to occasionally take upon themselves things that are unpleasant and disagreeable, in order that we may develop and retain mastery over ourselves. This is what the Orthodox Church encourages us to do through its emphasis on feeding the inner life through fasting and good deeds. Without self-denial and sacrifice there can be no real and positive dominion over ourselves.

October, 1973

THE JOY OF GIVING

It is often repeated, "It is more blessed to give than to receive." Thus blessedness, or happiness, becomes real joy the more one gives. Ironically, to give more of ourselves makes our own life all the more richer, for a shared talent is a talent that multiplies itself and is returned to us. In rendering help and service, for example, both the giver and the receiver are enriched, for that which we give away survives us. The Serbian people have a saying, *Radi onako kako te Bog uce,* which translates, "Do the things the way God teaches you." God has set the ultimate example in giving His only-begotten Son so that we may have joy and abundant life. Even nature knows the law of God, for we see that the good earth blesses us with the gift of crops with each and every passing year.

Following these examples, we are called to give of ourselves to others. We are especially called to give of our talents to God's Church, in return for all the blessings of life God gives to us. When we give to the Church we help build something that outlasts us, yet continues to bless us, in that our name is remembered and honored. While we are alive, we experience joy and happiness that regenerates our life.

There is a deeper underlying motive for all of this. A mother does not give birth to a child for the sake of obtaining some reward, but out of love. So, too, creation is what God's earth gives as a result of the Creator's established laws of nature. Moreover,

God sent His Son out of love for us. And so it is that St. Paul advises us, "and though I bestow all my goods to feed the poor, and though I give up my body to be burned, if I have not love, it profits me nothing (1 Cor 13:3). Our giving has to be done out of love.

January, 1974

I AM THE LIFE

Of the many pronouncements uttered by our Lord in the Gospels concerning the purpose and meaning of life, "I am the life" is perhaps among the most important. Life without a goal is like a ship tossed about on the high seas without any hope of arriving in safe harbor. How dreadful such a voyage would be. And what an empty life such would be as well.

Someone once observed that modern man is like a page torn from the middle of a book, with no ties to what went before and no sense of what is to come. Without a past and with no sense of the future, man loses all sense of belonging; he remains uprooted, lost, and terribly alone. This is the real malaise of today's society. By contrast, those who choose to become children of God are precious to Him. They find their place in the embrace of the Eternal One.

St. Paul affirms, "To live is Christ." Christ gave so much meaning to Paul's life that he could write, exclaiming, "Eye hath not seen, nor ear has not heard, nor has it ever entered into the heart of man what things God has prepared for those who love Him." Toward the end of his life he could say, "I have fought the good fight; I have finished the race; I have kept the faith. Henceforth, there is laid up for me the crown of righteousness, which the Lord, the righteous judge, will award to me on that day, and not only to me but also to all who have loved his appearing" (2 Tim. 4:8). We must establish a living, personal relationship with

85

Christ, who is "the Way, the Truth, and the Life," so that we may enjoy fully the purpose and meaning of life.

February, 1974

PARABLE OF THE SOWER

The New Testament shows us that not everyone is equally receptive to the word of God. In a parable that compares our soul to the earth, we find that the word sometimes falls on dry, packed ground so that it dries up and blows away or gets eaten up by birds. Others are like rocky ground, on which the seed of the word falls and sprouts, but dries up for lack of moisture. Still others are like weedy soil, in which the seed of the word is eventually choked out. Finally, there are those who are like fertile soil, upon which the seed of the word sown upon it springs up a hundredfold. What is sown upon us is what we will harvest. If the word in us is productive, then good will come our way. If we allow the word to dry up and die in us, then only bad will come our way.

Just as in New Testament times, so it is today. We must be aware of how we receive the word of God. Some people hear the word of God with a closed mind and heart. As a result, they remain lost. Some hear the word of God and receive it, only to abandon faith in God when difficulties and temptations arise. Still others hear the word and receive it, but after a time the cares and concerns, gains and rewards of the world suffocate it. Finally, there are the few who are likened to the good soil that receives the seed and helps it germinate until the plants are hearty and strong to produce a hundredfold.

Which of the above categories best describes the state we are in? God is the sower and will demand a harvest from every human soul, the fruits of which are faith and good deeds that lead to salvation and the Kingdom of Heaven. But it is up to us to choose what we will do with the word we have received. Why do so many choose slavery to the things of the world, losing sight of the harvest to come? May we receive the gift of the word freely given, choosing freely to cultivate it and bringing forth fruit a hundredfold and more!

June, 1974

THE SIGN OF THE CROSS

We make the sign of the Cross by joining together the tips of the thumb, index and middle fingers of the right hand, resting the two remaining fingers in the palm of the hand. In this position we then touch our forehead, chest, right and left shoulders, in that order. This action is followed by crossing our hands on our chest or allowing our hands to fall to our side as we make a bow. The thumb and fingertips together represent the three Persons of the Holy Trinity: God the Father, Who created us; God the Son, Who saved us; and God the Holy Spirit, Who abides in us, One God manifested in three Persons. The two remaining fingers in the palm of the hand represent the two natures of Jesus Christ, divine and human, united in one divine Person, represented by the palm of the hand. Thus, we make the sign of the Cross to participate in remembering God and all that He did for us.

Through the sign of the Cross we also express our response to the sacrifice of Christ. By placing our hand to our forehead we endeavor with God's help to know Him with our entire mind, reading and listening to the word of God. Bringing our hand to our chest expresses our desire to love God with all of our heart, receiving the Holy Eucharist as often as we can, as well as honoring every human being in fulfillment of the commandment to love one's neighbor. Finally, by crossing ourselves from the right shoulder to the left we promise to serve God with all our strength, in our personal life, in our family, in our Church, in our business, and in the community. This way we give expression to Christ's great commandment, "Thou shalt love the Lord thy God with all thy mind and with all thy heart and with all thy strength and with all thy soul." We bow to acknowledge that we are under God's dominion and rule. With the sign of the Cross we participate with all our being. It can be said that the sign of the Cross, as we Orthodox Christians make it, expresses some of the most basic and fundamental teachings of the Orthodox faith: the Trinity, the Incarnation, and the great commandment of Christ.

September, 1974

O COME LET US WORSHIP!

In the first part of the Holy Liturgy, when the priest enters the sanctuary carrying the Holy Gospel to the altar, the choir sings:

O come let us worship and fall down before Christ, O Son of God,
Who art risen from the dead, save us who sing unto Thee. Alleluia!

There before us is the icon of Christ, with those clear, steady, and all-seeing eyes, peering into our hearts beneath all of our insincerities, selfishness, impure thoughts and unkind motives. How dingy we must appear in His presence. Our self-made defenses, rationalizations, and justifications crumble before the honesty of His presence. If we come before Him in our pride, we are exposed for what we truly are.

It is then understandable why the Church sings this song and calls upon us to worship and prostrate ourselves before Christ. On certain Holy Days the words "Who art wondrous in His Saints" are inserted. The Saints provide us our example of how to worship with all of our being.

In prostrating ourselves before Christ we must first surrender our pride, the cause of a multitude of our shortcomings. It deadens our lives to the point that we become little more than "white-washed graves." Realizing this, we sing the words, "Who art risen from the dead, save us who sing unto Thee. Alleluia." It is indeed He who resurrects us from our weaknesses and death, resurrecting in us good works and a renewed life.

February, 1975

THE INNER LIGHT

Our Lord teaches us this: "The eyes are like the lamp for the body. If your eyes are clear, your whole body will be full of light; but if your eyes are bad, your body will be in darkness. So if the light in you is darkness, how terribly dark it will be" (Matt. 7:22-23).

Eyes are windows for the body. Without eyes, a significant aspect of the world's beauty is unavailable and every step can be a danger. There is no light, no color, no sighted recognition. But notice that in the second part of this passage it refers to the light being inside the person. With these words, our Lord turns the picture around, focusing on the light of the mind, soul, and spirit of the human being. Inner sight, or wisdom, depends upon light in order to see and recognize the law of God, for as it says in the Psalms, "Open thou mine eyes, that I may behold wondrous things out of Thy law." Our mind, having clear sight, chooses good things. Our thoughts, desires, and intentions are exposed to a field of light, healthy and directed to the service of God.

Without the inner life, man estranges himself from God. The light of the mind and soul is extinguished and confusion reigns. The body is overtaken by darkness and one eventually falls into the pit. This message is especially relevant for parents, teachers, leaders, and even clergy of God's Church, for if the spiritually blind lead the blind, eventually both fall into the pit. Those in positions of responsibility serve as eyes for those for whom they are

92

responsible. If those who lead are not able to see where they are going for lack of that inner light, even less will those who follow them be able to see.

July, 1975

THE STORMS OF LIFE

Matthew's Gospel relates two stories about storms on the Sea of Galilee (chs. 8 and 14). Both stories end with Jesus telling the disciples that without Him they can do nothing. St. Paul echoes this in his admonition, "Everything is possible for me with Jesus Christ, who gives me strength."

There is no one living who does not go through the occasional peril of drowning in a storm of trouble, but how many of us have reached out in faith only to discover that invisible hand from above that grasps us and delivers us to safety. Many of us have had this experience, and sometimes we also experience at some deeper level the quiet reproach from invisible lips, "Ye of little faith, why did you doubt?"

The Bible is full of great examples of those who acted on faith. Abraham was tested by God to offer his beloved son. Jonah, faced with death, said, "When my soul fainted within me I remembered the Lord and my prayer came unto Thee" (Jonah 2:7). Job lost everything, but called upon God and ultimately submitted to the mystery of God's ways. Last but not least, there is Daniel and the three men, who were thrown into the fiery furnace by the king of Babylon. In addition to these are the countless unnamed martyrs of the faith, including those of our own during the last wars.

When the perilous storms of life assail us, let us remember to call upon the name of the Lord; not only then, but also after He delivers us from them. Let us not despair from the occasional bouts with doubt that we sometimes have, for even the disciples Peter and Thomas began their lives in Christ with doubt. The Psalmist says, "In God I have my trust; I will not be afraid of what man can do to me. Thy words are upon me, O God; I will render praises unto Thee, for Thou hast delivered my soul from death. Will Thou not deliver my feet from falling, that I may walk before God in the light of the living?" More recently, the noted Russian novelist Dostoevsky said of his faith in Christ, "My Hosanna sprang from doubt." Finally, all those saints and martyrs, who certainly must have experienced the agony of doubt at times, won the victory enabled by their firm faith in Christ.

He is the victor in the Universe. He continually restores us from our human disorder. He replenishes us in our need, restoring our health. The blind see; the deaf hear; the mute speak. He is the victor over death; His order is life everlasting.

August, 1975

A CHRISTIAN HOME

The Christian home is the basis of our Church, just as the family is the basic unit of society. If home and family are not stable, civilization cannot help but reflect that instability sooner or later. If the Christian family gives up its responsibility, then there is simply nothing that can take its place. St. Paul advises Timothy, saying, "One that rules well his own house, having his children in subjection with all gravity, for if a man knows not how to rule his own house, how shall he take care of the Church of God? (1 Tim. 3:4-5).

People today usually blame society, including its schools, for troubles among our young people today. It is easy to blame the larger institutions of society, but it might be more telling to examine more closely what influences home and family have on persons who go off to these larger institutions for advanced learning. The home often falls short in fulfilling its responsibility for providing a safe and nurturing foundation. This great responsibility is expected even more of a Christian home.

If the home is loving, healthy, and stable, it will most likely produce loving, healthy, and stable persons who eventually come to participate in other societal institutions. The home, then, may be compared to a kind of spring that feeds fresh waters to rivers and lakes. What better source for this fresh water than the nourishing fountain of Christ in the Christian home.

How does one establish a Christian home? First of all, set aside a regular time, perhaps weekly, when the family can be together to share and renew its love. Second, establish Christian practices in your home: praying before icons, at meals, and before work; remembering and celebrating your slava, baptism, and marriage anniversaries; reading the Bible and edifying literature; and, above all, remembering the Lord's Day in your home, by first attending the Divine Liturgy at Church.

The Christian home is the primary place of training and nurture. For this reason it stands above other institutions of society including schools and even Church itself. One only has to look around to see the pressing need for renewal all around. So let it begin at home.

August, 1977

THE LIFE OF THE WORLD TO COME

"I look for the resurrection of the dead and the life of the world to come. Amen." These are the concluding words of our Holy Creed. This statement of faith is extremely important for us in that it affirms our belief in light of the fact that the present world will one day pass away. It is especially meaningful for us today, living as we are in an age when the threat of possible universal annihilation hangs over us. In addition to this, with so many emergent religious communities proclaiming the imminent end of the world, it is important for us to understand the teaching of the Church concerning the end of the present age.

First of all, we must accept the fact that one day the world will end. Ironically, this is something both scientists and theologians agree upon, although neither can say exactly when it will happen. Even our Lord, when presented with this question, answered, saying, "Of that day and hour no one knows, not the angels nor the Son of Man, but only the Father in Heaven" (Matt. 24:36). This message tells us to avoid the unhealthy desire to predict the end of the world at some fixed date, thereby frightening them needlessly into renouncing the blessings and responsibilities of the present world. Such an attitude is contrary to the world the Lord created, which the Christian faith affirms was created and pronounced by God to be good. Indeed there may be many signs that may be interpreted to indicate that the end is near, but just when that event will happen "no one knows."

For the Christian believer, the eventual ending of the world is experienced as the beginning of the Kingdom of God. It is a journey on the way to eternal blessedness. It is the inauguration of a better life beginning here and now. It helps us in avoiding sin to be ever mindful of our death and the "awesome Judgment Seat of Christ," but in doing so we find that the experience of death is simply one of passing as we continue on our spiritual journey in and toward Infinite God. Let us then stand together, looking ever for "the resurrection of the dead and the life of the world to come. Amen."

September, 1978

WHEN SHOULD WE PRAY?

We are accustomed to praying in Church on Sundays and holidays. We also pray when faced with sudden hardship. But to pray under everyday circumstances? Who has time? We are busy people these days. Yet it is possible to keep an open channel with God through the cultivation of an attitude of gratitude and rejoicing. As St. Paul reminds us, "Rejoice always," and "Give thanks in all circumstances."

We can learn to rejoice at all times by being aware of God's attributes of love and goodness, compassion and providence. We may expect great things through the grace of God from the treasury of His goodness. Our heart comes to sing for joy as life itself becomes our prayer. Living in the presence of God, His goodness becomes the experience of our lives.

Praying constantly may seem like an impossible challenge, especially when we must work for a living. But the apostle Paul was a working man, a tent maker by trade. He talked to working people and understood the necessity of prayer for sustaining a life of productive toil. The apostle instructs us to establish our priorities and seek the things that are from above, to love the things we ought to love, to focus our attention upon that which is worthy, and to embrace life as a glorious adventure in valuing and attaining the things that are truly good and valuable.

Much of our energy is devoted to things we think will make us feel good. Feeling good is not the answer ultimately, but in being a good person we participate in generating goodness, and from that true joy is obtained. If we value the highest and best, "seeking first the Kingdom of God and its righteousness," then our life becomes a living prayer and all necessary things come to us.

November, 1979

WHO NEEDS THE CHURCH?

The Church was established by Christ Himself for our benefit. The Church represents Christ in the world; it is His Body. All who are baptized into Christ "have put on Christ," that is, we are united to Him and become part of the Body of Christ in the world, with Christ Himself as its head.

Because the holiness and sanctifying power of Christ is present in the Church, we become partakers of grace by virtue of our participation in the Body of Christ. Some people assert that they can pray just as well at home and have no need for Church. This may be true, but there is a communal aspect to prayer that remains obligatory to fellow believers in terms of encouragement and accountability. After all, notice the opening words of the Lord's Prayer, "Our Father..." So what place could be more appropriate for uttering this communal profession of faith, taught from the mouth of our Lord, than the Church He established with His own blood?

It is truly difficult to see God and His purpose for our lives if we do not share our faith one with another. Who needs the Church? As members of the Body of Christ, we all do.

October, 1980

CHAPTER TWO

OUR CHURCH AND SAINTS

VIDOVDAN

Victory and defeat are but two faces of the struggle. Our spiritual history tells us that military victory is not always the true victory. Often victory proves to be the seed of decay and self-defeat. Ironically, as difficult as it may seem to understand, sometimes a defeat can ultimately turn out to bring a nation to a higher level of blessedness. Both faces of the coin are better viewed in the true light of Christian moral and spiritual values. If the victory measures up to those spiritual standards, then it is an authentic one. If not, then what appears to be a victory is self-deception and enslavement.

On the battlefield at Kosovo Polje, the Field of Blackbirds, the military defeat of the Serbs at the hands of invading Turks presented a tremendous challenge to the Serbian people, which endured a centuries-long period of intense spiritual self-examination under conditions of political slavery and oppression. The military defeat came about as a result of the greater physical might of the Turks, who maintained control over the Serbian people for over five centuries. But just as the Roman Empire conquered Palestine by force and ended up surrendering to the principles of Christianity, so, too, let us see what are the results of the battle at Kosovo Polje.

The invading Turks came to establish a vast political and military empire. They left their homes in Anatolia, Asia Minor, with the aim of subduing others through bloodshed and imposing the Turkish yoke upon the shoulders of formerly free peoples. The Serbs were such a people. Believing that God had given them their lives and their freedom, Serbs sought to defend their homes and their land, their ideals and their faith. Maintaining the conviction that everything they enjoyed was a gift from God, one wonders how any nation could rob another of the eternal gifts bestowed upon them by Immortal God. Our Serbian ancestors were spiritually and morally in the right. Their defeat at the hands of the Turks became a call for greater appreciation and safeguarding of the God-given gift of freedom. Guided by the principles and truth of Holy Orthodoxy, expressed through the leadership of the Serbian National Church, political emancipation was simply a matter of time.

Since that time, June 28, 1389, through the remembrance of Vidovdan, Kosovo has become the symbol of proven spiritual and moral values for an entire nation. The willingness of the Serbian defenders of faith and freedom to sacrifice their lives for something higher has become a national treasure for the generations that followed. Vidovdan means "Day of Sight." It represents the day in which the Serbian people gained a truer view of reality, that in its humiliation and defeat, it saw the higher light, the light of Heaven. We truly live only as long as these values are kept alive.

June, 1956

BLAGOVESTI (ANNUNCIATION)

The renewal of life is visible in nature beginning in early Spring, when the long winter frost releases its hold that brought life to a standstill. It is during this time of year, March 25th to be exact, that the Orthodox Church celebrates the Feast of the Annunciation (Old Calendar), the day that the Archangel Gabriel announced to the Holy, Most Pure and ever Virgin that she would be the Bogorodica, or Mother of God, whose coming was foretold by the Prophets.

"Hail, full of grace, the Lord is with you! Blessed are you among women!" said the Archangel to the Holy Mother of God. "Fear not," said the Lord's messenger. "You have found grace before God and you will be the Mother of the promised Savior of the world."

The words of this holy messenger were received by the Holy Mother with supreme and perfect loyalty and obedience, with the words, "I am the servant of the Lord. His will be done."

With this act the redemption of mankind began, therefore our Church places the Holy Icon of the Annunciation on the Royal Doors at the entrance to the Altar. This symbolizes our entrance into the Kingdom of God, following the example of the Holy Bogorodica, who carried the Eternal One in her womb, in her humble obedience to the providential Will of God.

Together let us recite the angelic salutation: "Rejoice, O Mary, full of grace, Virgin Mother of God, the Lord is with Thee.

Blessed art thou amongst women, and blessed is the fruit of thy womb, for thou has borne the Savior of our souls. Amen."

March, 1958

OUR PATRON SAINT NICHOLAS

All of our churches are consecrated to God and His Saints. Our own local parish is dedicated to St. Nicholas, who served as Bishop of Myra, in Lycea, a province of Asia Minor (present day western Turkey) in the early fourth century. This weekend we will gather to celebrate the 40th anniversary of our parish, at which time we will pray to God and thank Him that through His Saint we have been sustained and blessed.

Bishop Nicholas is celebrated as a renowned defender of the Orthodox faith, but he is also remembered for his kindness and generosity, as well as the working of miracles. Our celebration this weekend, called *Letnji Sveti Nikola*, marks the day on the Church calendar when the holy relics of St. Nicholas were transferred from the city of Myra to their present resting place in Bari, a city near the heel of the "boot" of Italy. St. Nicholas, whose primary day is celebrated on December 6th (Old Calendar), is the patron saint for approximately half of the world's Serbian families.

Miracles attributed to St. Nicholas the Wonderworker were not limited to his earthly lifetime. The miracle celebrated each May 22nd took place long after he fell asleep in the Lord. When the Saracens attacked his Myra, the city where his body had first been laid to rest, they left it in ruins. According to tradition, St. Nicholas appeared to an upright priest in Bari, imploring him to find his relics and bring them safely to Bari. This servant of God related his dream to the people and the leaders of the Church, who responded with joy and enthusiasm at the challenge. Emissaries were sent across the water to Myra. Searching through the ruins, they found the tomb of St. Nicholas. With love and care they exhumed the holy relics and on April 24th, transferred them safely to Bari, arriving on May 22nd. The clergy and the people of Bari received the holy relics with joy, placing them temporarily in the Church of St. John the Baptist. Three years later, a new church was built and dedicated to St. Nicholas the Wonderworker. His holy relics lie in the Holy Altar of that church to the present day.

By the prayers of St. Nicholas the Wonderworker, preserve us, O God, and save us.

May, 1957

TSAR LAZAR, MARTYR OF KOSOVO

Lazar was born in 1329. Following the death of Tsar Dusan, Lazar became ruler of the greater part of the Serbian Kingdom, successfully uniting Serbian provinces that were falling away in disunity at the time of his predecessor's death. In addition, Lazar healed the rift that existed between the autonomous Serbian Orthodox Church and the Greek Orthodox Patriarch, a victory that also helped consolidate the kingdom.

The education and well being of his people was one of Tsar Lazar's primary goals. Toward that end he founded a number of hospitals, churches, and schools. The famous Ravanica Church was one of his monumental institutions. In his letter of bequest to his church, Tsar Lazar writes:

> Following the examples of my predecessors, honorable kings and knights of the Serbs, I decided myself to place on the altar of God my sacrifices according to my abilities. Therefore I erected this monastery of the Holy Ascension of our Lord; I decorated the same and erected the buildings necessary for those who will dwell therein. Whatever I bequeath and give to this monastery was not taken from anyone, nor was it anyone else's property in any way, because I performed no hostility toward anyone and whatever I give was bought and paid for at the agreed price.

It was not long after this that the Turks attacked Serbia, defeating the Serbian army at Kosovo Polje ("Field of Blackbirds") on Vidov Dan, June 28, 1389. Tsar Lazar and other men of renown were taken prisoner and sentenced to die. Lazar was buried at Gracanica, in Kosovo, but after some time his relics were transferred to Ravanica. Still later, they were taken to Fruska Gora, where the other Ravanica church had been erected. Finally, during WWII Tsar Lazar's relics were rescued from Sremska Ravanica, which was demolished by the enemies, and transferred to Saborna Crkva in Belgrade, where they rest to this day.

Tsar Lazar is greatly revered by Serbian people everywhere for his personal faith, piety, and generosity. He led his people against tyranny and preferred the "Kingdom of Heaven" to a mere earthly kingdom when presented the choice, a response that became the national creed and ethic. The Serbian Orthodox Church has canonized the Holy Tsar Lazar and observes his day, June 28, or Vidov Dan, each year.

June, 1957

THE HOLY EVANGELIST LUKE

St. Luke the Evangelist was a follower of the Holy Apostle Paul. He was known for his scholarly training and his fine writing skills produced a gospel that was celebrated by all for the simple but artful profundity of its style. Attentive readers of the Bible who read Greek also see Luke's interests and style portrayed in the Acts of the Apostles, a companion volume that complements his gospel.

Luke met Christ in Jerusalem and was overwhelmed by His teachings. Finding the meaning he had been searching for, Luke followed Christ and, after the resurrection, the risen Lord appeared to him and Cleopas on the road to Emmaus, an event Luke recounts in his writings.

Following St. Paul's blinding encounter with the risen Christ on the road to Damascus, Luke became his inseparable companion in spreading the Gospel. Together they were most successful, for through their preaching and the work of other Apostles in the interest of salvation, the pagan philosophies and religions of the Greco-Roman world soon became fossilized.

According to Holy Tradition, Luke became Bishop of Thessalonica. He was a physician by profession, becoming a doctor of human souls as well. Some ancient writings attest to his skill in fine arts, specifically in the fashioning of Holy Icons. In his 84th year he was executed by hanging. His holy relics were stolen by the West during the Fourth Crusade (1204). Many Serbian families have St. Luke as their family patron, celebrating his day each October 31st. May St. Luke intercede for us!

October, 1957

SVETI SAVA

King Stefan Nemanja had three sons, of which Prince Rastko was the youngest. From his earliest youth Rastko manifested a deep love for learning and religion. While other boys his age played games or amused themselves in other ways, Rastko was seldom seen among them. He was often found standing quietly and listening to the wisdom of older persons. As a result, Rastko was able to express his crowning ambition early in youth. His entire being burned with a desire to enter the monastic order and become a monk. To many it was unthinkable that the son of a king should become a humble monk living in a monastery and enduring all the privations and hardships of an ascetical life. Nevertheless, Rastko nursed the burning desire in his soul by studying even harder and learning everything he could about his people, their life and religion.

When Rastko was about seventeen years of age, two learned monks on their way back to the monastery at Sveta Gora (the Holy Mountain - Mt. Athos) stopped at the palace of King Nemanja and begged for a night's rest. Rastko became very intrigued by these guests and began plying them with numerous questions about Sveta Gora, the monastic life, and religion in general. Sensing the young prince's deep interest, the monks answered all his questions in detail and more, much to young Rastko's satisfaction and gratitude. A few days after the monks set out to resume their journey, Rastko went hunting with his older brothers and their royal attendants. At dusk, when everyone returned to the palace from the hunt, young Rastko was not among them. An alarm was sounded and an intensive search began, but to no avail for the prince was nowhere to be found.

Wondering what must have happened, someone in the court remembered the visit paid by the two monks returning to Sveta Gora, recalling the rapt interest with which Rastko listened to their description of life at the monastery. Perhaps Rastko had run off to Sveta Gora!

King Nemanja dispatched messengers to the monastery at once. Sure enough, his son was there, having arrived at Sveta Gora footsore and weary in body but firm in mind and spirit in the dead of night. The brothers of the monastery had welcomed the young prince and had just finished bestowing monastic tonsure on him. Rastko's locks were shorn and in place of his elegant silk princely attire he wore the dark, solemn robe of the monks. The messengers were told that the young man had received the name Sava. Stunned by the experience, they returned to the king and reported all that they had seen.

From that point on, the life of Sava became in integral part of the history of the nation. His life and energy was dedicated to educating his people, building schools, churches, and monasteries. His exemplary life even influenced his father, for even King Nemanja himself eventually entered the monastic order. This is how young Prince Rastko became Sveti Sava, the patron saint of Serbian churches and schools, and why Serbs, wherever they happen to live, celebrate the Feast of Sveti Sava, honoring his life of dedication and revering his name.

February, 1960

OUR FORTY-EIGHTH ANNIVERSARY

This year we will celebrate the forty-eighth anniversary of our parish, marking the date when our fathers and mothers first dedicated our church to the service of God. This is the place where we have gathered for worship, practicing our religious customs and educating our children in the Orthodox faith. So you see, this place has become an essential part of all of us.

It is written in the Bible that, "unless the Lord sustains the house, all labor is in vain." Our faith in the Lord must be firm, for He is the one who will sustain us as He has done in the past. An anniversary offers an occasion to think about the past and to consider what we have accomplished. It has only been with the Lord's help that we have been able to succeed in our endeavors.

The future of our church depends upon the continued spiritual growth of all of its members. Each of us is asked to render our best in order to produce good results, for this is what God demands of us. As the Holy Apostle Paul writes, "Let them see your good works, and glorify our Father who is in Heaven." Therefore, let us continue the good work and ask the Lord to sustain His house. Let us also love one another.

Our Bishop, His Grace Firmilian, will be with us for our Slava. Won't you also please attend? Until then, may God sustain, bless, and love you all.

May, 1965

THE FEAST OF PENTECOST

The Church of Christ was born on the day of Pentecost. On that day in Jerusalem the disciples were "filled with the Holy Spirit and began to speak with diverse tongues, according as the Holy Spirit gave them to speak." For this reason we should remember that we are instruments of God's work upon the earth. The Holy Spirit dwells in the Orthodox Church until the end of time, discharging the power of God's grace through the Holy Mysteries of the Church, making holy every member who submits to God's will in this action.

Let us pray fervently that the Holy Spirit will come and dwell within us, strengthening us and our Holy Church by His presence, and let no man interfere with the works of the Holy Spirit. Christ has sent the Holy Spirit to us through His disciples as He promised. Through them we are recipients of the greatest gift God can bestow, for in Him is life.

June, 1965

OUR GOLDEN ANNIVERSARY CELEBRATION

Since the beginning of the year we have been planning the celebration of our parish's Fiftieth Anniversary, commemorating the beginning of our community's organized spiritual and cultural life. By most accounts, our celebration was indeed a fine and memorable event in the life of our church.

In addition to two days of social and religious festivities, we were presented with a beautiful Golden Anniversary Commemorative volume of the St. Nicholas Serbian Orthodox Church in Omaha, Nebraska, as well as a very fine Golden Anniversary Cookbook, prepared and issued by our Mothers' Club. For this festive occasion we were joined by all our friends and acquaintances from business and community, sharing our joy and being a part of this memorable event.

How did all of this come about? Only through loyalty to God and His Church, as well as to one another. As it says in the Bible, "Command the children of Israel and say unto them, My offering and my bread for my sacrifices made by fire, for a sweet savor unto me, shall you observe to offer me in their due season" (Num. 27:20). This indeed was our congregation's "due season."

This is how it was done: It was suggested that we organize a committee made up of two elected delegates from each of our parish organizations: the Circle of Serbian Sisters, our St. Nicholas Choir, the Mothers' Club, our Church School teachers and staff, SOTAYA, the Loyal Order of St. Sava, and the staff of "Omaha

119

Serbian News," all guided by the Church Board and its Pastor. Everyone gave of their best in this work, and it was crowned with success. Now that the event has passed, we see that our work was not in vain, for just look at what we discovered in ourselves:

1. We are capable of moving forward as an organized and unified whole, instead of groups acting out of their own self-interest;

2. We are capable of carrying out plans that pay good dividends;

3. We can organize a committee of just twenty people who can marshal the support of our entire congregation; and

4. With the help of God, we can accomplish whatever we set out to do.

There are seven months remaining in our fiftieth year, so let us continue the fine work we have started. Many thanks to all of you and may God bless you all.

June, 1967

SVETI SAVA

The Bible states, "Thou makest them princes on earth." How true this statement is concerning the importance of St. Sava for the Serbian Orthodox Church and people. For the Serbian people, St. Sava is what St. Patrick is for the Irish, St. Gregory for the Armenians, St. Denis for the French, or St. Anthony for Russia and in some ways even more, for the Serbian Orthodox Church is also called "Svetosavska," and Serbian Orthodoxy "Svetosavlje."

The Serbian Orthodox Church in the United States and Canada today has about 83 churches and four monasteries. Of these, 19 churches and one monastery are dedicated to God in honor of St. Sava. This shows the extent to which the Serbian people celebrate this saint.

The late Bishop Nikolaj says this about St. Sava:

> Once upon a time there lived a boy prince, very intelligent, rich, and fair looking. All the doors of worldly pleasure and success were open before him. But something within himself turned him away from all those things after which millions of human beings are feverishly striving. He renounced all vanities and allurements of the world and one day secretly fled away from the royal court and settled in a desert place as a poor stranger intent only on enlightening his soul by fulfilling God's will to perfection.
>
> Many years later this worldly prince, led by God's hand, returned from the desert to his native country as a prince of the church and forever the spiritual leader of his nation. Being childless, he became the father of many millions of his spiritual sons and daughters

throughout the centuries.

This happened over seven hundred and fifty years ago. And the torch of spiritual light he lit among his people is still burning and the number of his spiritual children in Christ is constantly increasing. He was sweet, but fearless; picturesque, but modest; most active, but calm; sociable, but lonely. He learned to know the art of right living in two worlds at the same time; a noble pattern emulated by many.

Each year on January 27th, on the anniversary of his death, we celebrate St. Sava's memory with special services and programs. In most of our churches, school children learn a small poem, or *deklamacija*, and recite it aloud. For many this occasion will mark the beginning of their public speaking.

Indeed, St. Sava's spiritual parenthood gave needed security, direction, and vision to the Serbian people and its Church, in times of peace and war, slavery and freedom, throughout history and to this very day. *Uskliknimo sljubavlju Savi*! Let us exclaim with love to St. Sava!

Date unknown

ABOUT THE CHURCH

We usually think of our church as little more than a building where we congregate in order to associate with others of our faith. For some, the world is the meeting place of two worlds: the visible one in which we live and the invisible one where we hope someday to live. An Orthodox church is designed and decorated to reflect a harmony of both worlds. It is the place where the human heart may reveal the best of its inner qualities, thereby coming into harmony with its Creator. Love towards God and human beings fills a heart with joy and brings wholeness to our lives.

The Apostle Paul reminds us that "Christ also loved the church and gave himself for it, that he might sanctify it and cleanse it with the washing of water by the word; that he might present it to Himself a glorious church, not having spot or wrinkle, or any such thing; but it should be holy and without blemish" (Eph. 5:25-27).

So, if such a Church is good for Christ, how much better would it be for us?

St. Irenaeus wrote, "Where the Church is, there is the Holy Spirit, and where the Holy Spirit is, there is the Church and grace." It clearly appears to us that Church is much more than a building or social gathering place. It is even far greater than what we as human beings could create, for it is of the Holy Spirit and God's grace.

We, as members of the Church, are obligated to do our work, but we do not determine the nature of the Church. That task belongs to Christ. The Church is holy because of her mission, sanctifying and extending grace to its members through the Holy Mysteries not because of any degree of sanctity among her members.

Let us all turn our eyes toward Christ and our patron St. Nicholas on this day, the celebration of our forty-ninth anniversary, that we may be sustained in prayers, steadfastness, and good work.

May, 1966

BUILDING OUR HOUSE

During the course of our entire life we work to create a life that can be thought of as a kind of house. It is the most significantly creative work we can do and all of us are obligated equally to fulfilling this responsibility. One can neglect this responsibility, but one cannot avoid it; neither can this responsibility be delegated to another.

The Orthodox Church and our faith stress the importance of this work. The Fathers and Mothers of the Church were living examples of this, which is why the Orthodox faith has survived many centuries of challenge and hardship.

Building the house which is our life means building up our character and bringing our personality into conformity with the image and likeness of God, for it is God who has designed the blueprint we carry within us. Christ, the master builder, is also the foundation of this house, sustaining us as we build. Christ provides the knowledge for bringing together the beauty and the usefulness of the plan, the same Christ who empowered the Saints of the Church to perfect their characters in Him. A sturdy building built upon a firm foundation can withstand any stress or strain that confronts it. How is our building? Is it strong and getting stronger? Or is it beginning to crack and crumble?

In the Sermon on the Mount Jesus points out the lovely stones with which we can construct a strong and beautiful house, namely purity, gentleness, courage, sincerity, benevolence, trust, and a passion for righteousness. These virtues of character and personality must be cultivated and developed. The plan of our Chief Architect includes rooms comprising an inner chamber of prayer, which is the sanctuary of the soul, and a living room of good works, with windows looking out on the glories of nature. Let us build the house of our life, using all the energy and skill that God provides.

October, 1966

PREPARING FOR OUR GOLDEN ANNIVERSARY

On the twenty-first of this month we will be offering up prayers of thanksgiving to God and our Patron Saint, St. Nicholas, for the existence of St. Nicholas Serbian Orthodox Church and her congregation. On that day we will remember in the parastos all those who labored, prayed, and died in faith of the resurrection. We will also be offering up prayers of joy for the opportunity given to us to organize and participate in such a pleasant and significant spiritual affair.

Our records show that since the building of our church there have been 132 weddings and 732 baptisms performed. We have also had 259 funerals. These numbers tell us that the during the fifty years of its existence, our church has performed its duty to her community faithfully and effectively. Our parish has endured many trying times, but with patience and understanding those problems were solved and the life of our church continued toward progress. This is a great lesson for us, which should not be forgotten.

As with life, our church is constantly changing. The people who were there to participate in the initial founding of our church are few in number among us. They have witnessed the changes that have occurred in our church over time, as well as the rapidly changing world at large. Through all of these changes, however, our faith remains constant and unchanging. In the work of the church across the nation, we see the sons and daughters of our "oldtimers" stepping up to their parents' former responsibilities. In our church here locally we have young, second and third generation Serbian American men and women filling positions of responsibility with eagerness and pride. The responsibility is ours; let us meet the challenge with temperance and prudence in all our endeavors and, above all, with faith in God. This will help us become even better as good Americans.

The Psalms remind us, "Behold, how good and how pleasant it is to dwell together in unity! It is like precious ointment upon the head that ran down the beard, even the beard of Aaron, that went down to the skirts of his garments . . . for there the Lord commanded the blessing, even life forevermore."

Working in the church we participate in God's work. "Take heed, therefore, unto yourselves, and to all the flock, over which the Holy Spirit has made you overseers, to feed the church of God, which He has purchased with His own blood" (Acts 20:28). May our children and our grandchildren remember this day in their old age. Congratulations and God bless you all.

May, 1967

APOSTOLIC SUCCESSION

The Church informs us that Jesus Christ gave the Apostles authority to teach and administer the sacramental life and to pass this responsibility on to others in an unbroken line of transmission to the end of the world. The bishops of the Orthodox Church, as the successors of the Apostles, have received this grace at their consecration, and our priests share in it when they are ordained. Thus, in our own day, the bishops and priests continue this same labor that Christ and the Apostles performed. How fortunate we are as Orthodox Christians to possess Apostolic Succession!

November, 1970

OUR CHURCH SLAVA
May 23, 1971

Our local St. Nicholas Serbian Orthodox Church belongs to the Midwestern Diocese of the Serbian Orthodox Church in the U.S.A. and Canada. The Serbian Church is a part of the global Orthodox Church that today numbers some 300 million Christians who are proud to belong to the Mother of all Christian churches.

Jerusalem is the cradle of Christianity. It was there that the Holy Spirit came upon the first Christian community. That part of the world is often referred to as the "East," which is why the Orthodox Church is sometimes called the "Eastern Church." The title bears witness to the origin and antiquity of the Orthodox faith.

As an individual desires to be distinguished in his life and work, thus preserving his identity, so, too, does a group of people. Our people living in the vicinity of Omaha and Council Bluffs did this by organizing the St. Nicholas Serbian Orthodox Church in order to preserve their faith and customs. The building site was purchased and the present church was erected in 1917, dedicated to St. Nicholas, the third-century bishop of Myra in Lycea (Asia Minor, modern day Turkey). Soon other organizations related to church life came into existence. The Circle of Sisters and the choir were organized in the 1930s. The present parish home was added in 1949. Then the Sunday School and Mothers' Club came

130

into existence. At one time our youth participated in a functioning "Youth Club," and later SOTAYA was organized to meet the needs of our young people. In 1946, our parish paper, *Serbian News,* was founded.

Concerned with its future, in 1968, our congregation purchased a new building site at 50th and Harrison Streets. We are now progressing with our work in hopes of realizing our goal of building a new community center and church there.

Reviewing the past, many of us will recall difficult and trying times when some lost sight of the faith and became lost themselves to church and community. But what a pleasure it is to listen to our old-timers who tell us about the many and various hardships and how they overcame them. When we compare our times with their experiences, they smile as if to say, "Do not worry. We have seen our dream come true under much harder circumstances. Have enough faith and you, too, will succeed."

With faith in God we will successfully meet our challenge. In the spirit of love and generosity, let us celebrate our church slava of 1971. Come, and bring your friends. Be a missionary for your church.

May, 1971

THE FEAST OF THE TRANSFIGURATION
(*PREOBRAZENJE*)

The Feast of Transfiguration presents the central idea of the Orthodox belief in all its mysticism and spirituality. According to our faith, our life is assigned to us to live and grow in Christ, being transfigured by grace.

Before His death, Christ took His closest disciples—Peter, James, and John—to a mountain where, the Gospel informs us, they saw a marvelous change come over Christ as He prayed. His face began to shine as brightly as the sun, and His garments became white as the light. It was the glory of God shining in Christ, shining in all its glorious splendor.

As they watched, the disciples saw Moses and Elijah, who represent the Law and the Prophets of the Old Testament, appear on either side of Christ. This affirms that Christ fulfilled the Law and the Prophets and thus enables us to be transfigured by the same divine grace that illumined Him as He prayed. In fact, at every Divine Liturgy a kind of transfiguration takes place in our life as we pray, sing, listen to God's Word, and partake of the Holy Eucharist.

We are informed in the Gospel how Peter desired to erect a sacred tent, or tabernacle, at the site of the Transfiguration. Surely we must pray and worship and remain inspired, but there is work to be done. There is still Christ's ministry of teaching and helping others that must be done. Although the Lord's Transfiguration is a picture of our own transformation in the glory of God, above all we are directed to listen to the words of our Heavenly Father, who on this occasion tells us, "This is My Son, listen to Him."

September, 1971

MOTHERS DAY

There is one vocation in this world exclusively for women, a calling upon which the existence of humanity depends, namely, motherhood. And in this country we set aside a day to set aside the demands of our busy routine in order to honor our mothers.

Victor Hugo tells the story of an event that happened during a war in France. A mother and her two children had been driven from their home. They wandered through the countryside for days, surviving only on roots and berries. On the third morning they sensed the approach of soldiers and immediately hid in the bushes. An officer ordered one of his soldiers to find out what was stirring in the bushes. He found the mother and her children cowering there and brought them out into the open. When the officer saw that they were frightened and hungry, he gave them a loaf of brown bread. The mother accepted it eagerly and, breaking the loaf into two pieces, gave one to each child. "Is it because she is not hungry?" the soldier asked his captain. "No," replied the officer, "It is because she is a mother."

Mother. The very word speaks of selflessness. Every true mother lives for her child. It is precisely that aspect of her love and devotion and sacrifice that calls for such a commemoration on Mothers Day.

The Orthodox Church has always celebrated great mothers. There would have been no great saints without them. St. John Chrysostom pays tribute to his mother, Anthusa, and St. Gregory the Theologian writes lovingly of his mother, Nonna. St. Basil the Great writes of Emelia and Macrina, "My understanding of God that I received as a child I learned from my mother and grand-mother."

America, too, has been blessed with great mothers. Abraham Lincoln said, "All that I am or hope to be, I owe to my angelic mother." When his mother died, Lincoln fashioned her a coffin out of wood and laid her to rest in the earth.

Thomas Edison said, "My mother was the making of me. She was so true, so sure of me; I felt I had someone to live for, some-one I must not disappoint." And the artist Benjamin West said, "A kiss from my mother made me a painter."

"Men and women frequently forget each other," said J. P. Bates, "but everyone remembers mother." Ralph Waldo Emerson noted that "men are what their mothers make them." And William Thackeray wrote, "Mother is the name for God on the lips and hearts of little children."

Kate Douglas Wiggen wrote, "Most of all the beautiful things in life come by twos and threes, by dozens and hundreds. Plenty of roses, plenty of stars, sunsets, rainbows, brothers, sisters, aunts, and cousins. But only one mother in all the world."

One may go on and on, quoting tributes to great mothers. God has depicted for us stories of many remarkable women in the pages of Holy Scripture, but towering above them all is the one to whom the angel said, "Blessed art thou among women, Mary full of grace," the Theotokos, Birthgiver of God, who is "more honorable than the Cherubim and beyond compare more glorious than the Seraphim." Standing there at the foot of the

Cross, gazing upon her dying Son, the Holy Virgin was remembered by Christ even at his last hour, turning to St. John, the beloved Apostle, and bidding him to care for his blessed Mother. In the final analysis, perhaps she is the inspiration for the celebration of Mothers Day.

May, 1972

SAINT JOHN, FORERUNNER AND BAPTIZER

St. John the Baptizer, celebrated by many of our Serbian families as their patron Saint *(Krsna Slava)*, was born the son of a God-fearing priest named Zacharias and his wife, Elizabeth, in a little town several miles from Jerusalem. On some icons he is depicted as an angel because of the nature of his holy life on earth. St. John is known as the Baptizer because he baptized Jesus Christ in the river Jordan. He is also known as the Forerunner because he called for repentance in preparing the way for the Lord (Mark 1:3).

What does it mean to prepare the way of the Lord? The prophet Isaiah describes it with these words, "Every valley shall be exalted, and every mountain and hill shall be made low" (Isa. 40:4). This means that the way of our lives will be made straight. Whoever confesses and repents, that person keeps the door of his or her soul open so that the Lord will enter in and bring life everlasting. Whoever is not able to confess his wrongdoings and feel contrition for them remains closed to what the Lord can do for him. In all cases, the ups and downs on the road of our lives are our sins and transgressions. God can take these away, or one may carry them all the days of one's life and experience a kind of death of the spirit as a result of them.

St. John baptized in the wilderness and preached baptism for the remission of sins (Mark 1:4). Thus St. John is the Forerunner because of his work and preaching, preparing the people for the way of the Lord. The state of our inner life testifies how significantly the Forerunner's call is for us today.

January, 1976

137

SAINT THOMAS

The Gospel read on the first Sunday after Pascha tells us about the disciple Thomas, the Apostle whose doubt and faith Christians remember. Hearing about the resurrection from the other disciples, Thomas replied that he will believe the story when he views Christ with his own eyes and feels the scars with his own fingers. As is said today, "Seeing is believing." Thomas demanded this after being with Christ during the performance of His miracles and even when Lazarus was brought back to life. Our Lord responded and presented Himself to the disciples while Thomas was with them. This is the way that God responds even to the request of one man, coming to him and showing Himself. St. John narrates this moment in his Gospel: A week later the disciples were together indoors again, and Thomas was with them. The doors were locked, but Jesus came and stood among them and said, "Peace be with you." Then He said to Thomas, "Put your finger here, you who doubt, and believe." Thomas answered Him, "My Lord and my God!" Jesus said to him, "Do you believe because you see me? How happy are those who believe without seeing me."

The name Thomas in Hebrew means double; in this case, not a twin by birth but double by nature. The great Russian author Dostoevsky wrote a novel titled *The Twins*, in which he depicts this aspect of human nature. Yes, there is more or less a twin in every man. The believer and unbeliever, at one and the same time trusting and distrusting. It is somewhat understandable, yet at the

138

same time comical, perhaps even pitiful, to see two human beings greeting each other with distrust before God who gave them life.

When our Lord showed himself to Thomas, Thomas exclaimed, "My Lord and my God!" showing that he accepted Christ as both God and man in one person. This contact gave Thomas the grace of the Holy Spirit and the renewal of life. We read in the Life of St. Thomas that he was condemned to death because of his heroic testimony of the resurrected Christ and that five soldiers pierced his body with their spears.

The Lord did not appear to Thomas just for the sake of the disciple, but for the sakes of all who seek truth and life as well, helping us to believe in Christ as the Resurrection and the Life. Even with this evidence there remains doubt in some corner of our minds. In order to enlighten this corner with the grace of the Holy Spirit, we must endure in prayer and be patient in waiting.

It is said that a stranger does not believe another stranger, but when faith is present then strangers become relatives, as brothers and sisters in Christ. When faith in God disappears, relatives revert to being strangers.

June, 1976

LET US DEDICATE!

On May 23rd of this year, with the help of God and our patron Saint Nicholas, we will dedicate our St. Nicholas Serbian Orthodox Church Community Center at 50th and Harrison Streets. On that day, we will be joined in this momentous event by our Diocesan Bishop Firmilijan; other clergy, both local and out of town; several Serbian-American friends from the region, including our sister parish in Kansas City, led by Proto Bajich, and friends from St. Louis. Pastors and parishioners from our local Orthodox churches will also be present to help us celebrate our dedication with joy: St. John's Greek Orthodox Church, St. Mary's Antiochian Orthodox Church, and Holy Cross Romanian Orthodox Church. Let us also mention the many friends from other faiths and traditions who have come with time and skills to help us.

It started with conversation, but soon became a dream. The desire to proceed with the plan actualized in 1968, with the purchase of land at our new location. Improvements were made and construction on the building began on June 29, 1974. Almost fully completed, we are now making ready to dedicate the structure to the service of God.

God has indeed helped us, even showing us how to secure financing for this undertaking. So many of our people worked hard to bring this about, through endeavors such as fundraising, making sacrificial donations, and countless other ways. It was heartwarming to see so many people working together, encouraging one another and completing the task.

What can I tell you now, but thank you for a job well done! But this is not enough; there is more, indeed much more. We must think of ourselves ten, twenty, or thirty years from now, even longer. We will hear the silent thank you from those who have gone ahead of us and watch with hope the generations we produce, that they, too, will preserve what God has helped us accomplish. This is our monument, resurrecting hope and life in our church for generations to come. There is work that remains to be done, loans to be repaid before we can say it belongs to God and us. Let us continue in prayer and work as we have done so far.

For our day of dedication remember that we are the hosts. Let us treat our guests with utmost hospitality and see that they are well taken care of, as our Serbian tradition of hospitality demands. Come! Bring your friends! Welcome! And God bless you!

May, 1976

PREPARING FOR THE HOLY LITURGY

Few things can be truly enjoyed without preparation. The trophy or medallion won by an athlete cannot be earned without first preparing him or herself through rigorous training and self-discipline. This applies to worship in the church as well. To enjoy the benefits of worship one must prepare oneself to receive them. All of us know that it is easier to sit than to walk, to read a comic book than read a novel, and for many to read a novel than read the Gospel. When Sunday approaches, a Christian can either experience church-going as a kind of chore through a lack of anticipation and preparation, or he or she can receive the full benefit and joy of celebrating the coming of our Lord, hearing His Word, and participating in the mysteries of His death and resurrection, receiving Him in the Holy Eucharist.

What does it mean to prepare oneself for the Holy Liturgy? Many people go out the evening before to eat rich food in a favorite restaurant or drink and listen to music. Often they come home late in the night after an evening of merriment and celebration. Those who do not go out might spend their time at home absorbed in some television program likely not conducive to spiritual or moral enrichment. Perhaps needless to say, preparing for church consists in none of these activities. Instead, try something different for a change.

The evening before the Liturgy, attend Vespers. If that is not possible devote some time to peace and quiet with your family.

That means leaving the television, that intruder into our homes, turned off. If you have an icon in your home, as Orthodox Serbs traditionally do, light the vigil candle and say a prayer with your family gathered around. Be moderate in taking food and drink. If one practices at least this much effort and self-discipline, going to church the next morning will be a joy instead of a chore. With such preparation everything will seem brighter and more peaceful and the question of when the Liturgy is going to end will not be first and foremost in one's mind. Instead, worship will become a joy and one will feel more a part of church.

September, 1976

ICONS IN OUR CHURCHES AND HOMES

Icons are inseparable from Orthodox faith and practice. The understanding and appreciation of icons brings one into the heart of the Orthodox Church. These images are not only representational, but presentational as well, in that they bring us into direct contact with heavenly realities. The icons themselves are not worshiped, for worship belongs to God alone, but icons are venerated for the spiritual reality they make available to us. They also show us that the world in which we live does not stand in opposition to the spiritual realm. Matter serves the spirit and through the spirit is transformed.

The word icon comes from the Greek *ikon*, meaning image. Since human beings are created in the image of God (Gen.1:27), then we, too, are icons. That is why during the Liturgy, when the priest censes the icons he censes the people as well. Thus the reality of the Incarnation is also affirmed in this way, for Christ Himself became the first icon.

The Orthodox Church is adorned with icons of Christ, the Mother of God, Prophets, Apostles, various Saints and Angels, and events like the Last Supper. With the help of these the faithful of the Church are united with the realm of the Kingdom of God. Past, present, and future all come together, as time enters into Eternity.

Icons have played a very important role in the history of the Orthodox Church. During the last century in Russia, for example, when churches were destroyed and all religious publications were banned and burned, some 5,000 churches and chapels remained out of 43,000. The iconostases of those remaining churches were the only instruments of religious education left in a vast land of people seeking meaning and help from above.

Every Orthodox home should therefore have an icon of Christ and, for Serbian Orthodox, an icon of their patron Saint. The power of the icon to transform the world around us is illustrated by the following story told by a soldier during the last great war. He tells how in the military barracks he was confronted by all sorts of banal and degrading, even pornographic, pictures displayed on the walls and furniture. As a Christian he found himself saddened and demoralized by them, so he decided to fashion his own image of Christ in the best way he could and placed it on the wall above his bed. Without a word about it being exchanged, one by one over time the degrading pictures began to disappear and eventually only his hand-fashioned image of Christ remained.

In many ways we have opened our hearts and our homes to banal and indecent influences, thus there is a need for us to have the Icon of Christ in our homes today. This is especially true for the sake of our children, who are impressionable to all sorts of influences in their formative years. So let God today miraculously transform our homes and our lives through the Holy Icons.

May, 1977

VJECNAJA PAMJAT
MEMORY ETERNAL

Vjecnaja pamjat, memory eternal, is the short prayer that closes the opelo, parastos, and pomen services, which call for laying to rest or remembering the deceased of our community. People may think that this prayer refers only to memory in this world, but as the late Bishop Nikolaj observes, the eternal memory is indeed eternal, for what gain would there be if one's name were remembered until the end of time but forgotten in Heaven? Thus it is correct to believe that in prayer we are commending those who have fallen asleep to eternal life in the Kingdom of God. That is the real meaning of *vjecnaja pamjat.*

The Bible tells us how the names of the righteous will be inscribed in the Book of Life, while the names of the unrighteous will be forgotten. In the story of the Rich Man and Lazarus, found in the Gospel of Luke, we see that the Lord pronounces the name of Lazarus, who enters the Kingdom of Heaven, but that the name of the rich man, prohibited from entering Heaven, is omitted.

Thus we see that the Church teaches and practices the eternal remembrance of our deceased faithful. We must bear in mind that countless numbers of people have passed through this life without noise or notice, but have received an eternal name in Heaven where neither death nor change exist. We are advised to bear this understanding in mind whenever we sing or hear this short but meaningful prayer.

March, 1978

OUR LIFE'S GOAL

Most of us are aware that we would like our lives to be meaningful. For that reason, many of us go off to school to learn a certain trade, preparing ourselves for a better life engaged in an endeavor we enjoy. The knowledge gained in schools has traditionally been called speculative knowledge, the kind of knowledge our society seems to value most.

What about the knowledge gained from life itself? We do not often think of this and many dismiss this experience as having any real value. Concern for this kind of practical knowledge is present in the Church, for the Bible expounds this reality on every page. This is the knowledge pertinent to the human soul and spirit and deals with the essential meaning of life. Without this type of knowledge, especially with its interest in positive moral values, we would not be able to establish or reach any meaningful human goals for our lives.

With preparation, learned skills, and a bit of luck, some acquire riches in this world. But what has happened to the riches of men? They have vanished from the earth without a trace. Even if someone managed to possess the entire world, it would not prevent the world from coming to an end, for riches cannot satisfy the soul's craving.

What is the goal of the human life? It can only be the Kingdom of God. The entire Gospel from beginning to end proclaims the coming of the Kingdom of God and heralds it as the only

147

meaningful goal in life. Without participating in the pursuit of this goal, we will experience only hardship. Many people focus on the wants and needs of the body and how to satisfy themselves in the present, but through neglect of the soul and spirit, they have died already to God and His Kingdom.

June, 1978

SVETA PETKA
(SAINT PARASKEVA)

St. Paraskeva is the patron Saint of our local Circle of Serbian Sisters and the majority of other such circles at Serbian churches throughout the United States and Canada. The venerable St. Paraskeva, known more popularly as Sveta Petka, is celebrated every October 27th.

Paraskeva was born at the end of the 10th Century, in the Serbian locality of Epivat (Pevat). Her parents were pious people who, in addition to Paraskeva, gave birth to a son, Eftemije, who became bishop of Tracea. Paraskeva was known as a pious and charitable woman who was often seen emerging from the Holy Liturgy giving gifts to the poor and needy, including among her gifts even her own cloak. She traveled to Constantinople and visited the Church of Hagia Sophia . There she received instruction in monastic life and eventually made her vows. As a monastic she made a pilgrimage to the Holy Land and settled in Jordan, leading an ascetical life similar to that of St. Elias or St. John the Baptist. In this manner St. Petka mastered the skill of complete control over all passions.

Sensing the coming end of her earthly life she returned to Constantinople and from there to her native Epivat. There she lived out her remaining years in ceaseless prayer and fasting. When she died, her body was transferred from there to the Church of Sts. Peter and Paul, whereupon many sick people came to receive miraculous healing through the intercessions of this saint. The following year, in 1238, Bulgarian Emperor Asen sent bishops from Bulgaria who transferred her body to a specially built church in Trnovo. When the Turkish Sultan Bayesit took Trnovo, the body was then transferred to Valacija (Wallachia), the southern part of Romania, and when this principality fell into Turkish hands, Serbian Tsarica Milica received approval from the Sultan to transfer St. Petka's holy relics to Belgrade. In the year 1521, Sultan Suleyman II took the holy body and transferred it to his residence in Constantinople, but upon experiencing a disturbing dream he turned the body over to Christians of the city. Moldavian ruler Vasilije Lupul (the Wolf) asked the Ecumenical Patriarch to give him the body of St. Petka. On October 14, 1641, the body was transferred to the Moldavian capital of Iasi (Jassy), in northern Romania and laid to rest in the city cathedral. As we can see, St. Petka was embraced by the peoples of Serbia, Bulgaria, Greece, and Romania.

The Church venerates St. Petka, along with other monastics, with this hymn: "You fell in love with the quiet life of the desert; you followed wholeheartedly in the steps of the bridegroom Christ, and took his tranquil yoke in your youth; you armed yourself heroically with the sign of the Cross against unseen foes; with the deeds of an anchorite: fasting and prayers; shedding tears you quenched the fires of passion, venerable Paraskeva; and now in the heavenly abode with prudent maids, standing before Christ, pray for us who reverence your venerable memory."

July, 1978

KRSNA SLAVA

Krsna Slava is our family "name day" in the spiritual tradition of the Serbian Orthodox faith, a kind of birthday celebration that stands alongside Christmas and Easter in importance for each family. Slava is the celebration of the patron saint of the Serbian home and hearkens back to the Christianization of Serbs by Byzantine Slavic missionaries. In bringing the gospel to the Serbs, missionaries Christianized existing religious practices by presenting Christian saints as protectors and intercessors for the family, thus replacing pagan deities who were believed to serve that domestic function. As a rule, the saint commemorated on or near the date of the family's baptism became the family's patron.

Although the missionaries probably did not think of it in quite the same terms, they were satisfying a psychological as well as spiritual need for their converts. The familiar sense of protection and support was met, but even more, families now had the living example of a patron saint for living a moral life in the Orthodox Christian faith. For that reason we hear among our people the ancient saying, "*Ko slavu slavi, tome slava i pomaze*" ("The Saint of a Slava will help whomever celebrates his Slava"). Through this tradition, the family gains even more assurance of safety and salvation in becoming united with the Holy Church, the communion of saints in the Body of Christ for which Christ Himself is the head.

Observance of the Slava is a distinctively Serbian practice. When two Serbs meet as strangers, the first question is often

"*Koju slavu slavis?*" or "What is your Slava?" Immediately a bond is established and they are no longer strangers. Such a practice played a vital part in preserving Serbian culture, situated as it was between the imperial influences and incursions of the Latin West and the Ottoman East. Even after five centuries of subjugation at the hands of the latter, Serbian cultural identity and hope was preserved through the Orthodox Church and celebration of the Slava.

Slava observance in the family is a joyous occasion. The home is open to all who would come in peace: relatives, kumovi, neighbors, and friends. The host does not sit down all day, but scurries about welcoming and serving. All are filled with joy in their readiness and desire to share the utmost in hospitality and friendship, sharing food and drink initiated by a prayer of thanksgiving. How many beautiful *zdravicas*, or blessings, are pronounced among them all. This is indeed a day of great rejoicing in the Serbian home.

Among the festivities, slava celebration participants observe the table near the icon on the eastern wall of the room, a kind of family altar upon which one finds a candle, the *slavski kolac* (slava cake), and *koljivo* (boiled wheat used in commemoration of the deceased). The icon is illumined by a votive candle that burns this day, as it does on every Sunday and holy day, in honor and commemoration of the patron Saint. At the Slava observance proper the candle is never blown out but extinguished with wine. The same wine glass is then passed around among the family members who each take a sip; thus symbolizing the continuity of the Slava. The *kolac* cake symbolizes Christ, the Bread of Life, and the *koljivo* is served in memory of the patron Saint and the deceased members of the family, whose names are pronounced during the ceremonial cutting of the cake. The aroma of incense fills the house, uniting the senses and the participants, body, soul, and spirit in this unique and festive occasion.

January, 1979

LIGHTING CANDLES

Why do we light candles and votive lights in our church and in our homes? Many people ask this question, continuing the practice without ever really knowing why. Bishop Nikolai, one of the most renowned authorities in our Church, explains this practice on the basis of the word of God revealed in Scripture, as well as through the Fathers in the Tradition of the Church

First, Bishop Nikolai states that we light the candles as symbols of the light of our faith, for Christ is the light to the world

Second, we are reminded of the character of the Saints, especially the Saints before whose icons our votive candles burn.

Third, the light of our candles serve to symbolize the dispelling of our dark deeds and mean thoughts. It is also our invitation to walk the road of the Gospel's light, thus bringing out the Savior's commandment to let our light shine before people, allowing them to see our good deeds.

Fourth, the candle is a small token of our sacrifice to God, Who sacrificed Himself for us. It is an expression of our gratitude and love for the one we petition in prayer for life, health, salvation, and the rest of the limitless bounty His heavenly love provides.

Fifth, the candle drives away the apparitions and dark powers that sometimes interfere with our prayers and draw our thoughts away from our Maker. These dark powers like the darkness and cringe whenever light assails them, especially when it is the light emanating from God through His Saints.

Sixth, candles remind us of courage and self-sacrifice. As the oil and the wick burn inside the votive light, so to do our souls burn with the flame of love in all sufferings, ever obedient to the word of God.

Finally, seventh, the lighting of the candle instructs us that, just as it cannot be lighted without fire, so, too, must the holy fire of God ignite our hearts. The virtues are our fuel, but it is the fire of God that lights them. Our life is a candle lighted at our birth, which is called upon to give off virtue until the end of its earthly life. So let us continue this beautiful practice, ever mindful of its rich meaning.

February, 1979

CHAPTER THREE

THE NATIVITY SEASON

A MESSAGE AT CHRISTMAS

The birth of God is a major event for Christians, Orthodox and non-Orthodox alike, all over the world. As we think of that event, which took place 1,955 years ago, we see two classes of men who were witnesses, namely, the shepherds and the wise men. As it was then, so, too, is it now. Our Lord is discovered by the simple and the very learned, but rarely by men with only one book, that is, the man who thinks he knows much.

The shepherds were simple souls who knew nothing of the politics of the world, neither its art nor its literature. Yet these simple shepherds knew more than kings, whose responsibilities include shepherding the earth, in being mindful of God above and the sheep at their feet.

The other category of men who found the Christ were wise men, not kings, but teachers of kings, searchers of the heavens and discoverers of wisdom in the stars. In science and religion the wise hold first place. For the proud man a star was just a star, but for the wise men it was the handiwork of God.

The teachable seek a teacher and the humble teacher seeks God. Both the simple shepherd and the wise man find God because they know that they do not know everything. The shepherds and wise men knelt together in humble adoration of the divine One, while King Herod himself could not find the baby he desired to kill. It will be of great benefit to us to emulate either of these types of men, humble shepherd or humble sage, in

159

our discovery of God. Their humility before God is an example and a call for all of us during this blessed Nativity season.

January, 1956

HRISTOS SE RODI!
Mir Bozji – Hristos se Rodi!
Peace of God – Christ is Born!

These are the words with which we greet one another during the Christmas season, words used in our Church since her earliest times. With this greeting we take time to reflect and reestablish the necessary harmony with God and among ourselves. What we mean when we think and speak about this peace of God is our inner peace, the peace of the human soul.

If we are to succeed in any kind of work, we prefer to do it in peace, for that is the only way we may concentrate and commit our best mental and physical faculties in order to work effectively. This means that our inner peace coordinates our best abilities. Imagine how much more organized and productive our life would be if we could increase the degree of our inner peace and be truly successful. People with this kind of inner peace are readily recognizable, for it radiates from their faces even as they work, and that is what first impresses us. For some of them, it took real work and effort to become that way and be able to lead a successful life. Take a sculptor, for example, who patiently works away at his project, first chiseling large chunks of marble, then refining smaller areas until he reaches the stage where he removes the dust with a swipe of his hand, revealing the beautiful image. To us, these are extraordinary people. If we want to follow their lead, we find that we, too, must remove many of the large and small obstacles from

161

our lives, in order to make a place for the inner peace that results from manifesting the image of God within us.

God loves us that much and wants us to have the best and to possess the greatest gift, the gift of inner peace, for the peace of God is the peace of the soul. We receive this gift by detaching ourselves, sometimes painfully, from the things that stand in opposition to God's peace.

God begins His mission with the message of peace: "Peace be to you," and finishes it that way, "May peace abide with you..." His birth was heralded by the angelic song of peace. Uttering those words God calls us to prayer, for as someone once observed, "Speak, move, act in peace, as if you were in prayer. In truth, this is prayer."

When we fall sick we follow the physician's advice to rest as much as we can in order to help our body overcome illness. By comparison, how much more meaning and significance do God's words carry? He knows infinitely more than we do about what it is we need and what is good for us. He is born and clothed in the body as one of us to show us the greatest example of life, love, and peace.

At this time, let us say, "God, I am living life in your peace. Do not let me ever become such a fool as to mistake anything else for our peace! Glory to You!" Having this inner peace, the true gift of the newborn Christ, we will be able to say, *Voistinu se Rodi!* "Indeed He is Born!"

January, 1960

ON HUMILITY

During the Lenten season of the Nativity we are reminded to cultivate humility through spiritual surrender to God, consciously placing all our interest, hope, and purpose completely in His hands. We find this important message grounded in the Bible: "Humble yourselves therefore under the mighty hand of God, so that he may exalt you in due time. Cast all your anxiety on him, because he cares for you" (1 Peter 5:6). This verse tells us that if we surrender to God's direction, guided by His mighty hand, He will help us to attain our true purpose and rise above our defeats.

With this in mind an early Church Father said that humility is the avenue to glory. Another Father reminds us that it was pride that changed angels into demons and that it is humility that turns human beings into angels. St. John Chrysostom tells us, "Humility is the root, mother, nurse, foundation, and bond of all virtue."

At this time let us learn and remember how to humble ourselves before God. Let us cast all our cares upon Him and be happy in the satisfying knowledge that He cares for us, all the while remembering that humility is the true avenue to inner peace and satisfaction.

December, 1960

HRISTOS SE RODI!
Christ is Born!

Glory to God in the highest, and on Earth,
Peace among Men of Good Will!

This is the song the angels sang in heralding the birth of the Son of God who was promised to mankind. The glory for this occasion belongs to God, for it was His will to send His Son, ushering in a new era for all mankind.

We should notice that all creation participated in this event. Humanity took part through Mary, the Holy Bearer of God, who gave birth to the child, nurturing Him who took on flesh. The world of animals was represented through their presence in the cave. Even the cosmos participated in that it was a star that led the wise men from the East, thus showing the humility of wisdom.

In addition to offering glory to God, the angels also invited men of good will to establish peace on earth. It is not the manner of God to force peace among the human beings He created, for Man and Woman were created as thinking beings and free. The angels called upon "men of good will," demonstrating that peace can come about only with a desire for peace through the investment of good will. Thus peace is determined by human will, that free human faculty with which we act upon our desires, directing our actions either for good or bad.

The human will is free, but in order to bring about peace it must be exercised in line with God's purpose, thus it is not the good will of a nation or a people of which the angels sing, but of the individual person, like you and me. Every person can be a center of peace and good will.

Peace is paramount issue in the coming of Christ. He is even called the "Prince of Peace." What sort of peace did His coming bring? It was the kind of peace that comes from restoring the link between God and mankind, and among humans themselves. Christ restored the connection between God and His creatures and healed the fragmented, lonely condition of human souls alienated from their Heavenly Father and from one another. When peace is restored, true prayer is possible, for in peace and silence we can hear the voice of God, the source of our life.

Has peace been restored to your soul so that you may hear the voice of God? Or is there a fluctuating state of alternating peace and turmoil raging inside, turning our hearts and souls into a battleground? In any of these cases we should mobilize our will to become good by inviting and upholding the peace that we are given through the grace of Christ Himself. Being Orthodox Christians of good will, let us celebrate the occasion of His coming by greeting one another with "Mir Bozji—Hristos se Rodi!" and singing the Blessed Nativity Hymn, Rodestvo Tvoje, Thy Nativity:

Rozdestzo Tvoje, Hriste Boze nas,
Vozsija mirovi svjet razuma;
Vnembo zvjezdan slucasci zvjezdoju cahusja,
Tebje klanjatisja solncu pravdi
I Tebje vjedjeti svisoti vostoka;
Gospodi, slava Tebje!

January, 1961

165

THE LOVE OF GOD WITHIN US

One of the hymns sung at Nativity Feast Matins reads:

> Our Savior has visited us from on high, from the east of easts; wherefore, we who are in darkness and shadows have found the truth, for the Lord has been born of the Virgin.

God created the world out of love and it is that same boundless and ongoing love with which He saves it. The challenge for mankind, created in the image of God, is to respond to that love and in the process move more fully into the likeness of God that we see in Christ.

Whenever we respond to the love of God, Christ is born in us. The clouds of darkness and shadows are pierced and dispelled, and our hearts are led into the light of truth. Thus our love in God manifests God within us and we are able to grow in Him more fully with each moment of our lives.

This experience of God is the only certain path for us. Before a person enters into this realization, he or she is deaf and blind toward the miraculous workings of God. Once the experience of self-realization occurs and the energies of God are working fully in us, we need no other miracle than that which has been born within our own souls; thus we should be open and welcoming of the presence of God within us.

The love of God born in us will also enhance our relationships with other human beings. Here is the usual cycle: A person pleases us in some way; we begin to idealize him or her; the person somehow fails us or does not live up to our expectations; finally, we become disappointed and lose our esteem for that person. The reason for this inadequate sort of human relationship is that our attitude is rooted within two false assumptions: First, that we ourselves are somehow above sin; and, second, that our neighbor is also sinless. How else is it that we severely judge and condemn those we expect to be more pious than the rest of us whenever one of them falls short of our expectations and commits a sin? The proper attitude challenges to love the sinner whether or not the sin was committed in knowledge or in ignorance. If the person sins out of ignorance, such a person still certainly deserves our love. If a person sins out of weakness and with knowledge, that person is rebelling against the image of God within and is still deserving of our love and pity, too. We are called upon to forgive endlessly, for we ourselves are in need of infinite forgiveness.

What is essential to remember in all of this, especially during this Nativity Season, is that the good that we value is born within us. Sharing the love of God, we can nurture and develop it more fully. Let the love of the newborn God find a response in our hearts, so that we may sing, "wherefore, we who are in darkness and shadows have found the truth, for the Lord has been born of the Virgin."

January, 1967

CHRISTMAS TRADITIONS

Through the customs and traditions celebrated by the Serbian people at Christmas time, we see how the birth of Christ is understood and celebrated. The Feast of the Nativity, as Christmas is properly called, is preceded by three weeks, each one dedicated to each of the personal roles of the family. The Sunday of the first week is called *Detinjci*, the day of the child. The second, *Materice*, is devoted to the mother. Finally, the third Sunday, *Ocevi*, is dedicated to the father. On each of these occasions, a custom of "ransoming" takes place, exercised first from the child toward the parents, then mother towards the children, and then father towards the family. The custom is to tie the designated person by surprise to some object. Their release is then secured by some gift, or "ransom." The practice promotes natural closeness and mutual appreciation among members of the family.

Another custom among our people takes place two days before Christmas, *Tucindan*, at which time a young pig is rounded up for the barbecue that takes place the following day in preparation for Christmas dinner.

On Christmas Eve day, called *Badnjidan*, the Yule log is selected for burning and the pecenica is prepared. The family gathers together for supper, which ought to be lenten, and a prayer is said by the father. Following the meal, straw is spread and gifts are exchanged.

Early on Christmas Day, the family attends the Holy Liturgy while the mother bakes the *cesnica*, a *pogaca* (round bread) made from wheat flour. It is traditional for the mother to hide a coin in the loaf. The person who finds the coin at the breaking of bread is said to have good luck throughout the coming year.

Mir Bozji! *Hristos se rodi*! The Christmas meal is the richest and most festive meal of the year. All the members of the family gather eagerly around the table. After calling the family to attention, the father lights a candle, censes the family with incense, and recites a prayer. Following this, the family turns the *cesnica* from left to right, singing the Christmas hymn *Rozdestvo Tvoje*. The *cesnica* is then broken and each person at the table gets a portion of the bread, with part of the bread reserved for the *polozanik*, or guest. This is followed with Mirbozenje, the practice of turning to the person on the right and having the older of the two say "*Mir Bozji! Hristos se rodi!*" ("Peace of God! Christ is born!") followed by a kiss on the cheek. The one returning the kiss responds with "*Voistinu se rodi!*" or "Indeed He is born!" The custom is not only enacted among the family, but after church services and among Orthodox friends that one meets on the street.

Thus the birth of Christ is observed in a concrete manner with the demonstration of the full meaning of this fact: Christ, the Son of God, is born and brings peace to all men of good will who believe in Him.

These are just a few of the more well known customs and traditions. There are many more, and these vary from province to province, but they share the central theme of Christ and His coming into the world. Christmas is followed with *Mali Bozic, Nova Godina, Krstovdan, Bogojavljenje*, and *Sveti Jovan Krstitelj*, again each with their own customs. Our traditions are rich in meaning and carry social and psychological, as well as spiritual benefits for the entire family.

December, 2003

CHAPTER FOUR

THE PASCHAL SEASON

HRISTOS VOSKRESE!

The Troparion for Pascha proclaims Christ's victory over death through His Resurrection. Thus it was death that died, not Christ. The Gospel tells us that on that first Pascha morning the women went to the tomb to embalm Christ's body, according to the custom of the time. The worldly authorities had posted a watchful guard around the sepulcher, lest someone attempt to steal the body. The greatest worry for the women was whether or not they would have help rolling away the large stone that sealed the opening. Even when they found that the stone had already been rolled away, they did not understand that He whom they sought had been resurrected. It was an angel who announced to them the Holy Resurrection, a message that inspired them more with fear than faith.

When the women carried the news back to the disciples, they regarded the words of the women as "idle tales and believed them not." Even when they saw the risen Lord, they thought Him to be a ghost. Mary Magdalene mistook Him for a gardener and the disciples on the road to Emmaus did not recognize Him until it came time for the breaking of bread. The Apostle Thomas doubted the report and would not be convinced until he put his finger into Christ's wounds. Taking Thomas's hand and placing it on His wounded side, Christ cured the Apostle of his doubt and he became the hope and healer of agnostics for all time.

Where do we stand? If the Apostles were expecting Him they would have believed it at once. When they finally believed, it took the sheer weight of indisputable evidence too strong to resist. They had to be convinced, and so were convinced for all of us. So now we stand with them in realizing that our former view of death was wrong. Christ is not dead, for death has been abolished. Moreover, Christ lives in us. If we believe this with all our heart, we may then enjoy full and abundant life in Him.

April, 1957

ON FASTING

"But this kind [of demon] can be cast out only by prayer and fasting" (Matthew 17:20). Such are the words of Christ Himself, spoken to His disciples faced with the disturbing challenges of evil. Through prayer our mind and spirit are directed toward God, while fasting leads the physical aspect of our being into conformity with our spiritual encounter with Him.

Christ teaches us the way in which we are to approach fasting: "But when you fast, put oil on your head and wash your face, so that your fasting may be seen not by others but by your Father who is in secret; and your Father who sees in secret will reward you" (Matt. 6:17-18). This places fasting in its proper perspective, seeing the action as performed for our sakes before God, who rewards us with many physical and spiritual benefits, producing a sound soul and body directed toward and serving its Maker. Following Christ's example, the disciples fasted before making important decisions, thereby commending fasting as an essential part of the Christian life (see Acts 13:25; 14:22; 2 Cor. 6:5; 11:27).

We are entering the annual forty-day period preceding Pascha, a time the Church sets aside for prayer, fasting, and repentance. During this solemn and holy season the faithful are invited to renew their heart and deepen their spiritual life by imitating Christ's retreat into the desert and by contemplating the events of His Passion.

March, 1960

175

THE FIRST SUNDAY OF LENT:
The Sunday of Orthodoxy

During the 8th C, a great struggle broke out in the Church over the use of icons in the worship of God. Because this dispute affected the whole of the Byzantine Empire, it became the primary issue of the century. The majority of believers stood firmly on the ancient Orthodox Christian practice of venerating icons, on the basis that the icons provide both a holy and educational role in the life of the Church: holy, because the lives and events of the Bible regarding Christ and the saints are presented; educational, because the main points in matters essential to Christian belief are also presented.

How important was this 8th-century decision to uphold the use of Holy Icons? For regions where Islam had overtaken formerly Christian lands, icons in the churches provided the only means of religious education for loyal Christians. In more recent times, in the Soviet Union, where religious publications are forbidden and Orthodox churches persecuted to the extent that over 38,000 churches and chapels have been destroyed and some 41,000 clergymen purged or sent away to die in concentration camps, Holy Icons in the remaining churches and secretly in homes provide the only education for loyal Orthodox believers.

The Church has established that the First Sunday of the Lenten season shall be set aside as the Sunday of Orthodoxy, a time when in our nation Orthodox clergy and people gather together

176

and celebrate the Triumph of Orthodoxy. It is also our custom that school children in particular prepare themselves for accepting Holy Communion on this Sunday.

March, 1960

ON THE RESURRECTION OF CHRIST

HRISTOS VOSKRESE! The Resurrection of Christ was the crowning event of all His wonders and provides the answer to the greatest of all human questions, namely, What happens after this life? What happens after the death of the body? What proof exists for the promise that Christ has vanquished death and that life continues in the Kingdom of Heaven? Meditating upon the Resurrection of Christ, a great mind once observed: "Our Lord has written the promise of Resurrection not in the Scriptures alone, but in every leaf of Spring."

Humanity was given the promise of salvation in Christ through faith, hope, and love—a life lived out by many who have found it the only real answer for a full and rewarding life. Inspired by the Gospels, Christian culture has achieved wonders. Some of our culture's achievements reflect the most profound truths of Christianity. For example, in recent decades, splitting the atom attests to Christ's truth that the elements of the physical world are changeable through the activities of science. How much more changeable are the elements in Holy Communion when through prayer and union with God we receive them from Him? The Church has been practicing this for almost 2000 years!

The Resurrection of Christ calls for all Christians to lift up their eyes toward Heaven to see resurrected faith, hope, and love. Through the burden of its many doubts, humanity appears to be

178

learning the hard way, exploring the universe in order to arrive at the truth of our need for help from Heaven.

Where human faith failed to believe God's promise, centuries of despair, toil, suffering, and destruction was the cost. Wherever love failed, the sickness of hatred made a harvest of the best of human efforts, demonstrating that the simple love of God among human beings provides the answer for perpetual life. Whenever hope was abandoned, doubt, treachery, and weakness was the cost.

Resurrection was necessary to assure mankind that we are not alone, that God is life, love, and hope, that life prevails over death, that God holds mankind and all creation in His hand, throughout time and all eternity. The Resurrection is the cornerstone of our faith, for as St. Paul states, without it our faith would be in vain (1 Cor. 15:17).

Another illumined mind has observed, "The diamond that shines in the Savior's crown shall beam in unquenched beauty, at last, on the forehead of every human soul, risen through grace to the immortality of heaven."

We need God's help to endure and remain steadfast in our belief. Blessed be the name of the Lord, henceforth and forever more!

April, 1960

179

A LENTEN MESSAGE

As we enter again the Lenten Season we are reminded to cultivate humility by fasting and praying, all with the aim of returning to our true selves as created in the image and likeness of God. This process involves surrendering ourselves mentally, physically, and spiritually, handing over all our interests, hopes, and purposes into the hands of God.

This important principle of living is described in the Bible:

> Humble yourselves therefore under the mighty hand of God, so that
> he may exalt you in due time. Cast all your anxiety on Him, because
> He cares for you. (1 Peter 5:6-7)

St. John Chrysostom, whose liturgy we celebrate, calls humility the "root, mother, nurse, foundation, and bond of all virtues." Yet this virtue is sadly lacking in the present age.

Let us learn to humble ourselves before God and walk the path toward Him with humility, fasting, and prayer. In return we will receive all His loving kindness and experience inner peace and satisfaction. Let us bow to Him on our knees in sincere humility and prayer, asking Him to forgive all the wrongs we have committed, repenting so that He may wash us in the showers of His grace, restoring us to communion with Him and with one another.

March, 1965

HRISTOS VOSKRESE! CHRIST IS RISEN!

The Resurrection of Christ is the cornerstone of the Orthodox faith. Unless we believe that Christ overcame death and rose from the tomb, our faith is entirely in vain, for as His life and death were real, so too is the reality of His resurrection. The troparion we sing during the Liturgy of St. Basil, in place of the Cherubicon, brings us into participation with this historical event:

> Let all mortal flesh keep silence
> and in fear and trembling stand
> pondering nothing earthly minded;
> for the King of Kings and the Lord of Lords
> cometh forth to the faithful.
> Before Him go the ranks of angels,
> with all the principalities and powers,
> the cherubim full of eyes and the six-winged seraphim,
> covering their faces and chanting their hymn:
> Allelulia, Alleluia, Alleluia!

On this day the Church instructs us to come to worship with these words: "Come, ye, take light from the light that is never overtaken by night. Glorify the Christ risen from the dead!" And in procession we sing the following:

To thy Resurrection, O Christ our Savior,
the angels in Heaven sing.
Make us also who are on earth
worthy to glorify Thee with pure hearts.
. . . This is the day that the Lord hath made;
let us be glad and rejoice therein.
Glory be to the Father and to the Son and to the Holy Spirit,
now and ever and unto the ages of ages. Amen

VAISTINU VOSKRESE!
INDEED HE IS RISEN!

April, 1965

HOLY WEEK

In the Orthodox Church, every Sunday of the year is a kind of "little Pascha" in that it commemorates the glorious Resurrection of our Lord Jesus Christ. During Holy Week, even the days of the week each have their own special significance.

On Holy Monday we remember Joseph, the son of Jacob who was betrayed by jealous brothers and sold into slavery in Egypt. After much suffering he came to triumph over his situation through faith in God, thus he is a prototype of Jesus Christ. The Gospel reading for the day tells about the barren fig tree, symbolizing the world's inability to bring forth fruit of its own, without the help of Christ.

The reading for Holy Tuesday presents the story about the wise and foolish virgins, as well as the condemnation of hypocritical scribes and teachers.

On Wednesday we have the story of the repentant woman who anointed Jesus Christ with precious ointment. Her action of selfless love stands in stark contrast to the greed and blindness of Judas, who betrayed the Master.

Great and Holy Thursday depicts the Last Supper of Christ with His disciples, at which time our Lord washed the feet of His followers. Here we also mark Judas's betrayal and the agony of our Lord in the Garden of Gethsemane. This drama unfolds in the reading of the Twelve Gospels of Holy Friday matins, read late on Thursday evening.

The Crucifixion and Death of Jesus Christ is commemorated on Great and Holy Friday. We enter the church, which has been darkened since the previous day, in somber prayer at the entombment of our Lord. Even so, it is important to realize that Christians already know the "end of the story" and anticipate the joy that is to come.

Great and Holy Saturday remembers Christ in the tomb during which time he made his descent into Hades, the realm of the dead. All week the bells of the church have remained silent. Holy Saturday begins with an attitude of mourning, but ends with joy and glory breaking forth during the matins of Resurrection Day, as "Christ is risen from the dead!" resonates throughout the church, as light and color and the sound of bells return.

April, 1982

CHAPTER FIVE

MISCELLANEA

THE ORTHODOX CHURCH[1]
Origin and Development

Christianity was born in the Middle East; so was the Orthodox Church. The region of Asia Minor and Greece were the first provinces of the Roman Empire, and there the first Christian communities were organized. The early followers were called *Christianoi*, from the word Greek word *Christos*, or Christ. From there Christianity spread further outward toward the four directions of the globe.

We do not have much information about the life of the early Church except what we read in the Acts of the Apostles. St. Paul, who had an understanding of Greek philosophy and the Hebrew Scriptures, made Christianity the universal religion. Known as the Apostle to the Gentiles, St. Paul began preaching with the support of St. Peter. Christian communities were formed in many places throughout Judea, Syria, and Galatia. These early churches kept in close touch with one another and the idea of the church as the one body of Christ was held by the early churches from the beginning. Visits between them were frequent and religious documents of various kinds were widely circulated. The Orthodox Church is the historical representative of these ancient apostolic churches.

One of the most interesting and imposing characteristics of the Orthodox Church is that, throughout the ages, its teaching, ritual,

---

[1] Excerpted from the St. Nicholas Serbian Orthodox Church consecration book Sept 17, 1989.

organizational structure, and dogma have remained true in every particular to its ancient original nature. Orthodoxy did not just develop; it has continually been won after a difficult and prolonged fight. It is seen today in various countries, among people determined to preserve and protect it without hesitation and compromise wherever inner freedom and its spirituality come into question. The noted Protestant theologian Ernst Benz concludes his book, The Eastern Orthodox Church, with the following statement:

> But in the deepest sense, the Orthodox Church itself sprung from the mystery of the Incarnation and, preserving that mystery in itself, sprouting in the wilderness as the church of ascetics, ravaged by the sandstorms of persecution, harassed by enemies of the faith, parched by immeasurable suffering and by inner and outer temptations, but yet unconsumed, burning with the fire of the Holy Spirit, aglow with the love of God, irradiated by the nuptial glow of the heavenly feast, illuminated by the all-transfiguring power of the resurrected Lord—the Orthodox Church itself is the Burning Bush.

BELIEF

The Orthodox belief is expressed in its creed and dogma. In the Orthodox Church, dogma and creed are not taken as "pure doctrine" on which the Church should rest. For the Orthodox, dogma and creed are seen as the divine and human process modeled upon the Incarnation of the Logos in the man Jesus Christ. The divine Spirit, proceeding from God, intervened in the history of human thought. The dogma has two aspects. In one aspect, its truths having origin in divine revelation, are divine, eternal, and unassailable. The other aspect, where the human mind is continually striving to achieve a deeper understanding and closer grasp of these truths, is human. Thus the dogma and the creed are a significant part of the liturgical life of the Church, not abstract formulations of "pure doctrine." They are found in hymns of adoration, in the rites of the baptismal service, and in the Eucharistic liturgy, where God is adored in the words of the creed just before the priest invokes the descent of the Holy Spirit. The dogma has fully preserved its original liturgical function in the Orthodox Church. The basic belief is that man is created according to the image and likeness of God (Gen. 1:27). God's image is given to man, but the likeness he has yet to realize. In this respect, Gregory of Nyssa, a Father of the Church (ca. 335 A.D.), wrote:

> O, You who are possessed with the desire to contemplate the true good, when you hear that the divine majesty is exalted above the heavens and that His glory is unfathomable, His beauty ineffable, His nature incomprehensible, do not despair of being able to see the object of your desires. . . You have only to return to the purity of the image established in you in the beginning: you will find in yourself what you seek, for once the spirit is cleansed and free from all wickedness, you will find the blessed vision in the serenity of your heart. There you will find purity, holiness, simplicity, all those gentle radiances of the divine nature by which God is seen.

Gregory continues further in addressing our likeness to God:

> By its likeness to God, human nature is made as it were a living image, partaking with the Godhead both in rank and in name, clothed in virtue, reposing in the blessedness of immortality, garlanded with the crown of righteousness, and so a perfect likeness to the beauty of the Godhead in all that belongs to the dignity of majesty.

The devotion to the dignity of man is expressed in the Divine Liturgy: "O God, who didst marvelously create the dignity of human nature. . ." Thus, any belittling of man is the belittling of God also. Orthodoxy has incorporated into its liturgy the various interpretations that the great ascetics have given it. Here are the three basic mysteries through which Orthodox spirituality can be grasped: the Mystery of the Holy Trinity, the Mystery of the Incarnation, and the Mystery of the Mother of God.

THE MYSTERY OF THE HOLY TRINITY

As Thou hast appeared to Moses in the thorn bush in the form of fire, Thou wast called angel, Word of the Father, who revealest Thy coming to us, whereby Thou plainly proclaimest to all men the tripersonal power of the one Deity. (Ernst Benz, *The Eastern Orthodox Church*)

THE MYSTERY OF THE INCARNATION

As the mysteries tell us, Moses foresaw in the holy vision Thine image: the thorn bush not burning in the fire, O Virgin, O sublime one beyond all reproach. For the Maker, dwelling in Thee, did not burn Thee who art elevated above all things made. Bride of God *(Ibid.)*

THE MYSTERY OF THE MOTHER OF GOD

Thou wert imaged long ago by the thorn bush on Sinai, which did not burn, O Virgin, in the touch of the fire. For as the Virgin thou didst bear. And exceeding all sense thou, Mother-Virgin, hast remained Virgin. *(Ibid.)*

Orthodoxy strives toward man's transfiguration according to Christ's example, and culmination is expressed in the Pascha

Troparion repeated several times on the day of Resurrection: "By His death He has trodden death beneath His feet." The joy of Easter is proclaimed, as is banishment of the ancient terror that beset the life of man. In this joyous mystery is the destiny of Orthodoxy.

THE SERBIAN ORTHODOX CHURCH

The Serbian Orthodox Church is a member of the family of the universal Orthodox Church. In the Orthodox family of Churches, the Serbian Orthodox Church enjoys the same status and equal rights with all other canonical Orthodox Churches, big and small. The same faith is being professed and the same canon laws adhered to while having its own jurisdiction to administer to the needs of its own flock. For this it uses its own resources and language. This is the ancient custom of Orthodoxy.

The founder of the Serbian Orthodox Church is Saint Sava (1173-1235). It was not coincidental that he went to Mount Athos and became a monk before going on to become the head of his Church. It was he who first gave himself to the service of God and His gifts. He dedicated himself to the service of God, not to isolate himself from the world and its people, but rather to actively serve God and His people. He freely gave in service what he himself had received. This is what made him to be remembered as the spiritual parent of his people and its Church. His Church was named *Svetosavska* and retains the name to this day. When we read about his life and work, we cannot help but detect his characteristics in his Church. He was a distinct personality and became God's instrument; so was his Church. His people, being geographically located between Byzantium in the East and the Latins in the West, became neither, but accepted Christianity and inherited the spiritual treasury of both, becoming more determined in history with other Christian nations. He was a Christian patriot who loved his people, respected all others, and shared their experience. It is a fact that his Church was never aggressive toward Orthodox or non-Orthodox peoples or their Churches, but rather continued in his example—to give love and full care to its people in all situations until this day, overcoming all obstacles that lay in its way.

Serbs became Christian in the eighth century. The process began in the seventh century, and by the ninth century, liturgical books were translated into their own language. The process of Christianization was slow. Success came when Christianity was preached to the people in their own tongue; Christianity became their religion. To the Christian religion of love and resurrection they gave their youth and hope. This gave birth to the transfigurative national and personal code of ethics expressed in the famous Kosovo epic. This gave power and moral stamina to Serbs that allowed them to withstand a five hundred year period of slavery. The famous German poet Goethe learned the Serbian language in order to read the Kosovo epic. Jacob Grimm composed the grammar of the Serbian language.

There are twelve million people in the Serbian Orthodox Church, which is governed by the Patriarch, Holy Synod, and the Council of Bishops. The Serbian Orthodox Church in the United States of America and Canada is canonically part of the Mother Church, but enjoys full administrative autonomy. The church congregations are governed according to the principles of the original church communities, where Christian harmony is the goal for all its members. For this purpose, each individual church member is responsible to bring out the best quality of his or her inner being and establish communion and harmony with other members. This is essential for the presence of God's Spirit. Here the spirit of *Sabornost* is represented.

A TURNING POINT OF FAITH

The famous Russian intellectual Alexander Solzhenitsyn records in his works that one day, sitting on a bench in the *gulag*, or Soviet work camp, despondent and deep in thought, he and a fellow prisoner contemplated suicide. Looking down at the ground in front of himself he saw in the dust what appeared to him to be the sign of a cross. It was at that moment that a turning point occurred in the life of this great man; he decided to turn to the Orthodox faith of his parents and ancestors.

THE RINGING OF BELLS

When the communists took power in Russia and anti-religious propaganda became the rule of the day, many churches were closed down and a number of them were converted to other uses. Priests and bishops were put in jail or deported to the *gulag*, or work camp, to the tune of some 43,000. Astoundingly, only about 3,000 survived; still, the devoted Orthodox believers continued to ring the bells faithfully on every Sunday or other Holy Day. That was an outward sign of faith in God that was being expressed in those days.

THE SIGN OF THE CROSS

The Cross is foolishness to those who do not accept Christ, but to the Orthodox, it is the symbol of great glory, signifying our redemption and God's great love for humankind. It has been said, "Without the Cross there can be no Resurrection," for the realization of true life in this world cannot be separated from suffering.

We commemorate these great mysteries every time we make the sign of the cross. Let us, therefore, make the sign of the cross with the greatest reverence, reciting the accompanying words and prayers with utmost devotion.

SPIRITUAL BLINDNESS

Christ teaches us in the Gospel that physical blindness can be cured if it is His Holy will. More importantly, however, is Christ's power to heal another kind of blindness, which too often afflicts Christians today, namely, spiritual blindness. How many people walk in the darkness of sin and grope aimlessly for satisfaction in sinful pleasures that do not satisfy? Satisfaction and real pleasure lies someplace else. It lies in creativity and the effort to do good continually in the life given to us. Unfortunately, many a person chooses satisfaction in pleasures that bring only temporary joy and leave a lasting regret. Pray that our eyes may be opened to an understanding of the spiritual treasures of our Orthodox faith.

ORTHODOX EDUCATION

By educating our children in the Orthodox faith and tradition, we aid them in living a life with a firm foundation and a sheltering roof over their heads. At the same time, we secure a future for our Orthodox faith and Church.

Christ said that we must not prevent little children from coming to Him. Certainly, the educational policy of the Orthodox Church has always been to emphasize to the children the truth of our faith. Our children of today are the Orthodox leaders of to-morrow. No cost or effort is too great to provide them with sound religious education. Support your church school and teachers by bringing your children, worshiping, and working.

INNER PEACE AND BODILY HEALTH

We are reminded not to overlook the fact that our health does not depend on food alone, but on inner peace as well. To have this peace our life must be centered upon God. This life in God, cutting us off from worldly turmoil, brings peace to the heart and, through this, keeps the body in good health as well.

THE REASON FOR OUR COLDNESS

We grow cold when our heart becomes distracted from the things that really matter. Our relationship with other people falls victim to coldness and when it invades family life it is tragic in-deed. This condition develops when our heart becomes absorbed in the things of the world. Forgetting God, our heart becomes enslaved to the world. We begin worrying about different things, getting angry and blaming others, becoming discontented and following the impulses of a wandering heart. We must stand guard against these things, only then will the coldness diminish and then can we regain the original warmth of our heart.

AS THE TWIG IS BENT...

As we prepare to open our parish school for religious instruction, we should recall what a tremendous responsibility and privilege Orthodox parents and teachers have. Nowhere can spiritual leadership be found to have more lasting value than that which is received in the Christian home. Roughly two centuries ago, Alexander Pope wrote, "As the twig is bent, the tree is inclined." Christ said, "Suffer the little children to come unto me." He knew that the direction the twig is bent determines the fate of the tree, and that the way a child is trained determines the kind of man or woman he or she will become.

This is the time of the year to make a fresh beginning in our church school. With God's help we still need three elements in order to succeed: parents, children, and teachers. If one of these is missing, the whole program will be limping.

Date unknown

PRAYER AND HUMILITY

Prayer is essential for the healthy life of the church. Prayer should mark the beginning and end of everything we do. It should inform and inspire our decisions, our work, and our shared activity. Without prayer, the church grows cold and empty, degenerating into a confused and aimless wondering about what should be done next. Shouldn't we then appreciate the power of prayer and the divine guidance it provides for our lives?

Prayer has an amazingly beneficial effect in the inward self, keeping the mind and heart turned in the right direction. It compels us to work in harmony with God's will and has the power to bring us back to the person we were meant to be. Prayer thus leads us to be humble.

Humility is a necessary quality for remaining within God's approval. The great teacher of the Church, St. Augustine, writes, "Should you ask me 'what is the first thing in religion?' I should reply that the first, second and third thing therein—nay, all—is humility." We read the words, "Gird yourselves with lowliness of mind." Being truly humble means that we do away with our pride and our high mindedness. Humility opens the doors to divine grace in our lives. Indeed, it works miracles. This was depicted in the Bible by the proud Syrian army chief, Naaman. In order to be cured of leprosy he had to exercise faith and humbly obey the instructions of Elisha's attendant to bathe himself seven times in the Jordan River. This kind of humility brings grand blessings that the proud can never experience and enjoy.

Date unknown

ISAIJE LIKUJ!

This hymn, "Isaiah, Dance for Joy," is sung in our church at weddings and the cutting of the *Slavski Kolac* (Slava cake), along with two other hymns. Isaiah was a prophet in Israel during the 8th Century B.C. His name, which in Hebrew means "God saves," seems to reflect some kind of challenge to faith that Jehovah would save His people not only from political disaster, but from evil of every kind. Under the reign of King Ahaz, Isaiah proclaimed, "Therefore the Lord Himself will give you a sign. Behold, a young woman shall conceive and bear a son and shall call him Immanuel" (Isa. 7:14). Immanuel means, "God with us" (Manojlo, in the Serbian tradition). The prophecy, which was meaningful in its own time, also foretold the coming of the Messiah, fulfilled when Christ was born of the Virgin Mary more than seven centuries later.

Through the birth of Christ, the love of God toward the human race was fully manifested. In order to save the human race, God became incarnate, taking on human flesh. Because marriage has the purpose of promoting life, the Church finds it appropriate to sing "Isaije likuj!"—Isaiah, dance for joy!--to remind the newlyweds of the holiness of matrimony and the providence of God in the giving of children. It also serves to remind the couple of the majesty of God, that they may keep their eyes affixed to the higher spiritual and moral meaning of their marriage.

The other event at which this song is sung is during *Krsna Slava*, a religious custom of the Serbian people. During this feast the *slavski kolac* is cut during the singing of *Isaije Likuj*. This is done remembering that Christ referred to Himself as "the Bread of Life" and "the Bread that comes down from Heaven, that a man may eat of it and not die" (John 6:48-51). Thus we may eat of the eternal Bread of Life, our spiritual food.

Date unknown

FINDING OUR TRUE SELVES

We must look to ourselves for the cause of the greatest part of our unhappiness. Many of us want to be happy and have the respect of others, but often we do not behave in a way that brings these things about. Most damage is done when we try to be someone or something other than what we truly are, that is, a person created in the image of God, or try to possess something that is not ours to have. Losing control over ourselves, we begin trying to control others. Not knowing our own true measure in life, we begin expecting everyone else to "measure up." But if other people can see us in that unnatural state, cannot God see us as well?

This is what we are called to correct, namely that unnatural state that results from subverting the original goodness into which we were created. When we reflect the likeness of God in our image, then we have "come back to ourselves," experiencing again the life and joy that we were created to enjoy as children of God.

Date unknown

DEADLY GOSSIP

The great enemy of Church life is gossip. Gossip may be compared to the tares that grow and suffocate the seed, which is the Word of God. Yet, it is a truth that the element of gossip in many instances takes precedence over prayer in the lives of some people in the Church. It eats deeply into the life of the Church and, in many cases, tears away the fabric of the Church by alienating persons from God.

Prayer is the main cure for this condition. To be with God means to pray constantly. We must practice active prayer in order to counteract and overcome the damaging effects of gossip. If someone is tempted to indulge in gossip, let him first say the words, "Lord Jesus Christ, Son of God, have mercy on me." If we are serious about healthy Church life, then we must practice prayer and avoid gossip.

AN EXCERPT FROM *SO HELP ME GOD!*[2]
SUMMER OF 1941

In the summer of 1941, one could look around the country-side to see fields that had been either partly cultivated or not at all. The places where corn had been seeded were left without cultivation against the ravages of weeds. The hayfields near the houses remained unworked. (The job of mowing the hay usually required ten or twelve workers a couple of days to complete.

Mowing the hay was a job I enjoyed as a young man. Each of us was expected to keep pace with the man in front, to avoid frustrating the man behind. The job required more skill than that which was needed for the cultivation of corn. One had to know how to use the rub-stone for sharpening the scythe, and the quick pace separated the men from the boys. For these reasons, the job paid better than cultivating corn, and it was understood that better food would be prepared for the hearty workers. Generally, a lamb would be prepared for the main dish. If the weather was threatening, we would gather as much as we could, fighting as long as possible the coming winds and rain. To view the results of this work was sweet, and the pleasant aroma experienced during the cutting of the hay gave way to the pungent smell of drying hay.

Now the fields were beginning to show their ripened, golden color. We had no harvesting machines then, and even if we did,

2 New York: Vantage Press, 1992, pp. 131-36

we would not have been able to use them on such small and scattered parcels of land. We had only our sickles to brandish in our fevered, steady pace with one another. The new rows of sheaves would appear behind us harvesters. The weather during the winter wheat harvest was usually hot. Cold water was brought in a *brema*, or wooden container, which would remain cool for some time. Every few hours we would pause to rest in the shade of a fruit tree. Generally, the workers were young or middle-aged. The most beautiful thing about all this, however, was to hear the songs of the workers, raised loudly as they marched into the fields at sunrise and out again at sunset.

The harvesting of autumn, ending with the corn harvest, also holds special meaning for me. It was then that I felt alive in the fullest sense of the word. But alas, these beautiful seasons would now be different than any other our region had ever known. This year, no work would be done, neither would the happy songs of the harvesters be sung. There would be no time for joy, for the fear of our lives replaced our joy, even quenching any romantic yearning. No one spoke; we were all preoccupied with other things, like staying alive.

I remember our little stream where, during this time of year, swarms of children could always be found. They especially enjoyed playing near our *vir*, or eddy. This is where I learned to swim in the earliest days of my life, for every summer day of my grammar school years I could be found here. Mother would call us for dinner from the south veranda of our home. We could fish both east and west, upstream and down, sometimes angling and other times reaching for fish with our hands, under slippery stones and tree roots. Sometimes we encountered fishing competitors under the stones, that queasy feeling of encountering some long, rough, and slow-moving creature, which caused an immediate shiver and a hurried escape from that primordial terror only a snake can evoke. Our catch of fish would sometimes be quite good, but Mother usually declined from cooking our catch on particularly hot days, when neither she nor we could be sure how long the fish had been out of the water. As for me, I could never eat my catch; I found it repulsive. But now, this fateful summer, even this place was abandoned. Where had everyone gone? Even if I knew the answer, it was often too difficult to bring to mind.

Sometime around the middle of June, we could hear explosions in the distance; they were barely audible, but unmistakably it was the firing of cannons that we heard. No one dared investigate whether this was test firing going on or something else. One was not in a position to conduct such inquiries.

It was sometime around June 22 that news arrived that Germany had launched an attack upon the Soviet Union. Like the rest of the world (although we didn't know it at the time), we were puzzled by such an event. After all, hadn't these two countries just signed a friendship pact? In fact, during Hitler's attack on our country, our own local communists had greeted the oncoming Nazis as liberators!

Ironically, though, such news brought some encouragement. It was somehow comforting to know that things were still occurring on the international scale and had not stopped with our defeat. Yet the first news from the eastern front was discouraging. Many of the people who favored this latest development were those whose fear of communist domination obscured any view of what the Nazi plan for world domination was all about. With a broad, sweeping front, Hitler's armies advanced rapidly into the Soviet Union. News came that the Ukrainian front had collapsed and that Soviet soldiers were surrendering in huge numbers.

In our region, meanwhile, things seemed to settle down somewhat, as the newly created NDH began to take control of things. For a short time we no longer heard of private or public executions. We even began to see people working in the fields, but the fear of the unexpected still loomed foremost in our hearts and minds.

*   *   *

During the second week of July, on a beautiful, sunny day, a coach stopped in front of our house. It was Nedim! What a pleasant surprise to see my friend. He was not alone, however, for climbing down from the coach behind him was a young Moslem man, then a civil engineer, whom I recognized. I was surprised to see him with Nedim, for in our small group of Aca, Nedim, and me, we had never really associated with this man at all. Nevertheless, I was pleased to share this visit.

My parents were always happy to have visitors. My mother began preparing food, while the rest of us sat down at the table. Nedim began the conversation by teasing me about hiding in the village while things in town and the rest of the country were back to normal. They had come to tell me that there was no longer any reason to fear and so today they had come to take me into town. They told me that they had made plans for an outing and that they wanted me to go with them. My father sided with them and began to insist that I accompany them.

Soon dinner was ready and we settled in to eat. My brothers were in the wheat field, getting ready for an early harvest. After the meal, we got into the coach and headed toward town. We had traveled only a few kilometers when I noticed some work that was being done in a field that belonged to us. I don't know just what it was that came over me, but I asked the coachman to stop. I climbed out of the coach, muttering to my companions that I suddenly felt obligated to enter the field and assist in the making of hay. My friends were surprised by my behavior, but so was I. I felt uncomfortable but stood firm in my decision to stay in the fields near the village. My friends sat in the coach for a while, then proceeded toward town. My parents were surprised to see me when I arrived home after a hot, dirty day in the field. I was not able to give them a sensible answer as to why I had refrained from going into town.

I learned later on that, on that day, Nedim and Aca were thrown into prison. This was the last I heard from them...

In the final days of July, the constant thunder of cannon fire could be heard in the west, beyond Mount Grmech. As with everything else, we had no idea what was going on. Who was firing, and at whom? Were the shots from training maneuvers, in preparation for being sent to the eastern front? Or were they warnings to us? No one knew.

OUR LAST SUPPER TOGETHER

Coming home at dusk once for my usual supper before withdrawing for the night to the field south of our house, I noticed the dark silhouette of my father, sitting alone near the chopping log. He saw me coming and, always happy to talk with me, asked me to sit down. His shirt was wet with perspiration, from both the heat and the fact that he carried a little extra weight. He told me that perhaps he had been somewhat brash in his response to my inquiry about escaping to Belgrade. He was concerned about reproaching me and advising that I stay to suffer the fate of the family. Now he was saying that he wished I had followed my original plan, for then I would at least have some chance of advancing myself. Then he fell silent. After a few moments, I excused myself for supper and went into the house. A half hour later, as I was on my way out to the field, Father was still there, sunk deep in worried thought.

The next evening before sunset, somewhat earlier than usual and without any previous planning, we all arrived at the house for supper. As we ate, a wagon rolled to a halt in front of our house. Two men came to the door. They were armed but greeted us politely. The men were brothers from a rather prominent Roman Catholic family in Ostra Luke. They apparently knew my father, who offered them chairs and plates of food. They placed their guns near the table beside them and sat down. As they were removing their caps and shoving them into their pockets, I noticed the bright letter U that had been sewn into each one.

My older brother Branko motioned to me to step outside with him. I remained at the table, avoiding his eyes. Suddenly the elder guest spoke up, saying that they were to escort our father to the *opstina*, or city hall. They said that they were doing this for his own personal protection and that they were acting as friends of our family just trying to do their best for us. After a few minutes,

Father stood up. He looked as us as if to say that there was nothing for us to be concerned about. When he finally spoke, he told us that there was no reason to worry, since our guests had promised that he would be home again in the morning. Saying that he would see us soon, he left with the brothers. This was the last time we ever saw him.

My brother Branko, I remember, reproached me the next day, saying that we should have acted. I did not ask him what he thought we would have been able to do about it. After expressing his assurance in front of all of us, in addition to the brothers' promise that they would guarantee our father's safe return with their lives, we had little choice but to hope for the best. We spent the whole of the next day waiting, but Father never came home.